Series Editor Scott Miles

D1586859

Effective
Reading

Jackie McAvoy

2

Pre-Intermediate

MACMILLAN

Macmillan Education
Between Towns Road, Oxford OX4 3PP
A division of Macmillan Publishers Limited
Companies and representatives throughout the world

ISBN 978-0-230-02915-6

Original design by Designers Collective
Page make-up by Designers Collective; Julian Littlewood
Illustrated by Anthony Hope–Smith; Designers Collective; Ed McLachlan; Vicky Woodgate
Cover design by Designers Collective
Cover illustration/photograph by Designers Collective

**The authors and publishers are grateful for permission to include the
following copyright material:**
Extracts from *The Legend of Sleepy Hollow* and Rip Van Winkle (Macmillan Reader) retold by
Anne Collins (Macmillan Heinemann ELT, 2000), copyright © Anne Collins 2000, reprinted
by permission of the publisher.
Extract from *Black Cat* (Macmillan Reader) by John Milne (Macmillan Heinemann ELT, 1975),
copyright © 1975, reprinted by permission of the publisher.
Quoted interview with Graham Holliday, copyright © Graham Holliday, reprinted by
permission of the author www.noodlepie.com.
Quoted interview with Ben Curtis, copyright © Ben Curtis, reprinted by permission of the
author www.notesfromspain.com.
Use of the name Zorb ® granted with the kind permission of the manufacturers, www.zorb.com.

These materials may contain links for third party websites. We have no control over, and are not
responsible for, the contents of such third party websites. Please use care when accessing them.

**The authors and publishers would like to thank the following for
permission to reproduce their photographic material:**
Bloomimage p104; **Corbis / Reuters** p50; **Corbis / Zefa** p60; **Digital Vision** pp11, 25,
73, 74, 91, 96; **Firstlight** p6; **ImageBank** pp65, 68; **ImageMore** p48; **Image Source**
pp14, 15; **Image State** p101(t); **Jacqueline McAvoy** p101(b); **National Geographic** p24;
PhotoAlto p37; **Stockbyte** p42; **Stone** p78; **Superstock** p32; **Taxi** pp55, 86.

Whilst every effort has been made to locate the owners of copyright material in this book,
there may have been some cases when the publishers have been unable to contact the
owners. We should be grateful to hear from anyone who recognises copyright material and
who is unacknowledged. We shall be pleased to make the necessary amendments in future
editions of the book.

Printed and bound in Thailand

2018 2017 2016 2015 2014 2013 2012 2011 2010 2009
10 9 8 7 6 5 4 3 2 1

"*Reading is to the mind what exercise is to the body.*"

Richard Steele: *The Tatler* 18th March 1710

Contents

1 Culture Shock

PRE-READING 1   **Answer the questions.**

1 In which country do people eat with a fork in the left hand?

   a America

   b Britain

   c They both use a fork in the left hand.

2 Are some American accents very different from British accents?

   a Yes, very different.

   b Yes, but only in a couple of places in the States.

   c No, not different at all.

3 Do you think that American universities have a lot of clubs you can join?

   a Yes, they have a lot.

   b No, they only have a few.

   c No, they don't have any.

PRE-READING 2   **Complete the paragraph about a student magazine with the words or phrases in the box.**

advice   culture shock   ~~magazine~~   settling-in   social life

ABC is a student (**1**)_*magazine*_. Every month there is news and information to help students with both their (**2**)_____ and studies. The magazine also gives help and (**3**)_____ to new students to make (**4**)_____ easier. This month there are suggestions on how to deal with (**5**)_____.

Read about foreign students living and studying in the USA.

Cultural differences

Studying in a foreign country can be exciting. It can be difficult too, especially if the culture is very different from your own. However, there are often surprises, even if the culture is very similar. When Megan, a British student, first arrived here in the United States she
5   knew that Americans ate their food with a knife and fork. 'But they don't use the knife and fork like we do,' says Megan. 'In Britain we eat with the fork in the left hand and the knife in the right hand. Whereas Americans often just use a fork in the right hand.'

Megan is also surprised that Americans tip a lot more than the
10 British do. 'We never tip a waiter just for a cup of coffee, but Americans tip 15 per cent. The accents can be so different, too! I'm slowly getting used to everything.'

For students who come here from more different backgrounds, settling in can take longer. Kit-ken, a student who came from
15 Taiwan only a few months ago, told us 'When I first arrived everything was new and exciting. I really liked the differences between here and home. I was happy to be in a new country. Now, though, I miss my family and friends and feel a bit lonely. Sometimes I'm confused about what to do. There are still lots of
20 things that I like, but now there are more things I dislike. I feel really homesick!'

For advice we turned to some students who now have few problems about being a student here. Seydou arrived from Senegal two years ago. He told us 'Kit-ken shouldn't worry, this is perfectly normal. I
25 felt exactly the same as she did. I didn't understand the culture and my English wasn't improving, either.'

Seydou realised this was because all his friends were from his own country. 'So I decided to get to know some North American students, and other international students. I went to the student
30 union where there are a lot of different clubs. There are sports clubs, dance clubs, clubs for people who have the same religion, clubs for people who want to find out more about something – there are loads! I saw there was a club for students interested in music and so I joined that. It made all the difference! I made friends quite quickly,
35 and I was able to understand the culture a bit better. The students were interested in me, too. We talked about the differences, and I began to feel a lot happier. We now get on well and often hang out together.'

40   Miguel from Mexico added, 'My main problem was the food. I really missed eating my favourite dishes! Cooking for myself was also hard and I ate too much fast food, which was not good for me. Then I found a Mexican restaurant nearby. Now I go there quite a lot, and I often take other students to give it a try. Also my mum sends me packages with Mexican food in them, and that really helps, too.

45   Understanding a new culture is important, but it's good to have things from home, too.'

Seydou sums up the advice for us, '…'

COMPREHENSION 1   **How does Seydou sum up the advice? Choose the best comment.**

1   Things will get better if you stop talking to people from your own country and eat only North American food.

2   Culture shock is normal. Meeting people from other cultures is a good idea, but having things that you know and like also helps.

3   Culture shock is not normal. There are doctors at the student union who can help.

COMPREHENSION 2   **Answer the questions.**

1   Which sentence is correct about line 1?

a   Being a student in your own country is easy.

b   There are always problems being a student in another country.

c   There are good and bad things about being a student in another country.

2   In line 12, another way of saying *I'm becoming more familiar with the differences* is _____.

3   In line 18, what does Kit-ken say about her family and friends?

a   She tries not to see them.

b   She doesn't want them to know she feels alone.

c   She feels sad because she isn't with them.

4   In line 20, how does Kit-ken feel?

a   She feels ill because she's far from home.

b   She feels sad because she's far from home.

c   She feels ill because she doesn't like her new home.

5   In line 22, what is another way of saying *to go to someone for help*?

6 In line 24, what does *this* refer to?

    a He didn't understand the culture and his English wasn't improving.

    b feeling homesick

    c His friends were from his own country.

7 In line 34, which phrase means *that changed things for the better*?

8 In lines 39 to 43, which of these sentences about Miguel are true?

    a He has a problem with Mexican food.

    b He didn't cook in Mexico.

    c He ate a lot of fast food because it's his favourite type of food.

    d He sometimes goes to a Mexican restaurant on his own.

    e He sometimes goes to a Mexican restaurant with other Mexican students.

COMPREHENSION 3   **Friends are very important! Complete the sentences with the verbs in the box. Use each verb only once.**

miss   turn to   make   get to know   get on with   hang out

1 I think I _____ Sam because we both like the same things.

2 It's difficult for me to _____ new friends because I'm very shy.

3 Joining a club is a good way to _____ other students.

4 We mostly _____ with the other people in our music club.

5 When I'm away from home I really _____ my friends.

6 If I have a problem I know I can _____ my friends; they're always ready to help.

get to know

hang out

Grammar	Indefinite article (*a / an*): to talk about something for the first time; to talk about jobs
Articles	*You can eat food with **a** knife and fork.*
	*Megan is **a** student.*
	Definite article (*the*): to talk about something again, or when there is only one
	*British people eat with **the** fork in **the** left hand*
	No article (*Ø*): to talk about things in general
	We don't tip waiters for coffee but Americans do.

GRAMMAR 1   **Complete the sentences about the second part of the text with *a*, *an*, *the* or *Ø*.**

For example:

Seydou is __*a*__ student at __*an*__ American university.

1 He went to _____ student union at his university.

2 He saw there was _____ club for _____ students interested in _____ music.

3 It helped him to understand _____ culture better.

4 Miguel found _____ Mexican restaurant near the campus.

5 His mum sends him _____ packages.

GRAMMAR 2   **Are the articles in these sentences about Kit-ken correct?**

1 Kit-ken thought __an__ advice from Seydou was very good.

2 She likes acting and __ø__ films so she joined __an__ film club.

3 She got __the__ main part in __a__ film about __ø__ student life.

4 Now she wants to be __the__ actress in Hollywood!

SPEAKING   **Talk to a partner and answer the questions.**

1 What problems might foreign students from your country have when living in the USA?

2 What problems might students from the USA have when living in your country?

3 Can you give some examples of problems foreign students might have with the culture or customs of your country?

Effective • *Skills*

ACTIVATING
VOCABULARY

Match the verbs (1–6) and nouns (a–f).

1 have   **a** into tears

2 blow   **b** in a pub

3 give   **c** in coloured ink

4 drink   **d** lunch

5 burst   **e** a present

6 write   **f** a whistle

Six foreign students had cultural problems when they studied abroad. Can you guess which countries the students were in?

Doing things differently

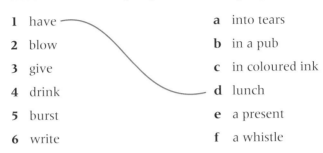

A   I was a student in _____. One day, I was invited to a local student's home for dinner. I wanted to take something special for his parents so I took an expensive bottle of wine from my country. However, when I gave them the present my friend was quiet, and looked embarrassed. When I asked him why, he explained, and I felt   5 embarrassed, too.

B   Well, I was a student in _____ and one day I crossed the road. Just that! Suddenly I heard a whistle blowing and a police officer came running after me. He said, 'You must wait at a crosswalk and only cross if the 'walk' light is on.' He was very angry with me and I burst into tears!   10

C   When I was a student in _____, a local friend invited me to have Sunday lunch at her home. During the meal, my friend said to me, 'Put your hands on the table.' When I looked, I saw that all her family had their hands on the table, except me. I had no idea why!

15 **D** One sunny day, when I was a student in _____, I went to a pub with two local friends. We all had a drink but, because I was so thirsty, I drank mine very quickly. My friends still had half-full glasses so I bought another drink, just for myself. My friends said, 'Hey, you can't do that!' and then I felt cheap.

20 **E** I spent a year studying in _____. I was shocked the first time I went to a lecture. At the end of the lecture I stood up to leave, but sat down again when all the students started knocking on their desks. I asked another student, 'Why are you knocking?' It seemed a strange thing to do.

25 **F** I love making my own birthday cards. One day, when I was a student in _____, I decided to make a card for a local friend. It was in different colours and I thought it looked lovely, but when I gave it to her she cried, 'Oh no! My name is written in red ink!' When she explained why, I felt terrible.

GENERAL UNDERSTANDING **Match the problems above to one of the explanations below. Complete the text with the correct country.**

1 In France, it's polite to eat with your hands on, not under, the table.

2 In Jordan, where most of the people are Muslim, many families don't have alcohol in the home.

3 In Korea, a name written in red ink means that the person has died.

4 In the USA, crossing the road in the wrong place is called *jaywalking* and in some cities it's illegal.

5 In Germany, students don't clap their hands to show they like something, they knock on their desks instead.

6 In the UK, when you are in a pub, you buy drinks in *rounds* – for you and your friends, not individually.

READING FOR DETAIL **Which student had one of the following reactions?**

For example:

Which student started to cry?   _The student in the USA._

1 Which student didn't understand the problem?   _____

2 Which student was very surprised?   _____

3 Which student felt really bad?   _____

4 Which student was uncomfortable with what his friend thought?   _____

5 Which student felt bad about not buying something?   _____

SPEAKING Talk to a partner and answer the questions.

1 Which foreign student do you think had the biggest problem?
2 Can you think of a time when you did something wrong in a social situation?
3 When was the last time you were embarrassed? What happened?

PRONUNCIATION Find the 11 words in the text. Decide in which words the underlined *-ed* ending is pronounced like:

| 1 /t/ watch<u>ed</u> | 2 /c/ smil<u>ed</u> | 3 /ɪd/ want<u>ed</u> |

For example
invit<u>ed</u>   _3_

1 want<u>ed</u>   ____
2 explain<u>ed</u>   ____
3 embarrass<u>ed</u> ____
4 cross<u>ed</u>   ____

5 cri<u>ed</u>   ____
6 shock<u>ed</u>   ____
7 start<u>ed</u>   ____
8 seem<u>ed</u>   ____

9 decid<u>ed</u>   ___
10 look<u>ed</u>   ___

WRITING Look at the following sentences:

Do: In the USA, cross the road at a crosswalk.

Don't: In France, don't eat with your hands under the table.

A foreign student is coming to your university. Write some dos and don'ts about your culture.

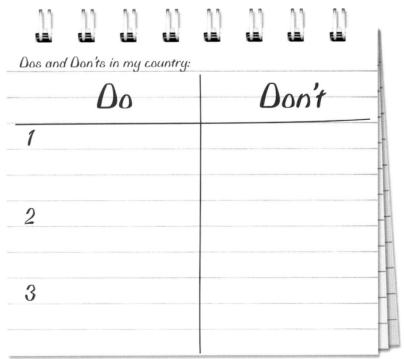

Dos and Don'ts in my country:

Do	Don't
1	
2	
3	

2 Gum: something to chew on

PRE-READING 1 **These words are from the text. Before you read, fill in the missing letters.**

For example:

I **want some chewing gum! Do you have a s** *t i c* **k?**

1 An imaginary friend is not a r _ _ l person.

2 I can't remember your name; I have a terrible m _ _ _ _ y.

3 My sister got top grades again: she has a great b _ _ _ n!

4 Students taking exams are under a lot of s _ _ _ _ s.

5 Does your heart b _ _ t faster whenever you see Ziyi Zhang?

PRE-READING 2 **Tick (✔) the suggestions you think are good advice for students preparing for exams.**

1 ☐ Eat small amounts of food (snacks) between meals.

2 ☐ Drink a lot of coffee.

3 ☐ Study at night.

4 ☐ Study in a quiet room without music.

5 ☐ Don't get too comfortable.

6 ☐ Exercise during your breaks.

7 ☐ Chew gum.

8 ☐ Chat with other students during your breaks.

Read the advice for students who want to do well in their exams and compare your answers to Pre-Reading 1 and 2 with the text.

Chewing for a better grade

Without doubt, chewing gum is very popular. Annual sales of gum in the USA, for example, are over $2 billion. But perhaps this is not surprising when you learn that Americans on average chew about 300 sticks of gum per person a year. Worldwide, the Wrigley Company sells more than $4 billion of chewing gum each year – that's a lot of gum!

Why is chewing gum so popular? One manufacturer says that it not only helps you relax more, but it also helps you to stay awake. This is the reason why the American armed forces have given chewing gum to their soldiers since the First World War. People also chew gum after a meal to have fresh breath. It can help fight tooth decay, too, which may mean fewer visits to the dentist.

But do you know that there's a better reason for chewing gum – it can improve memory! Do you have an exam coming up? Well, revising is obviously a good idea, but scientists say that chewing gum can help, too.

How do scientists know that chewing gum can help memory? The scientists divided 75 people into three groups. One third chewed real gum, one third chewed imaginary gum, and the last third didn't chew anything at all. Then the scientists gave each group different memory tests to do. The results were very interesting. The people with real gum did better than the people with imaginary gum. And the people with imaginary gum did better than those who didn't have any gum at all.

How does chewing gum help memory? One possible reason is that when people chew there is more activity in an area of the brain that is important for memory. Another possible reason is that when people chew their heart beats faster, and so more oxygen goes to the brain. However, the three groups all worked at the same speed. They could all work out the answers quite quickly. Scientists say this shows that chewing gum doesn't help you to concentrate better.

Meanwhile, study experts in Chicago are trying to help students who are taking exams, and chewing gum is included in their list of tips. They say that students are under a lot of pressure to get good grades, and so they often do the wrong things when revising for exams.

40

45

Many students, for example, eat unhealthy snacks between meals. They also drink a lot more coffee and study until very late at night. This means that when they take their exams, many students are tired and unhealthy. The experts suggest that students should exercise during their breaks, or chat with friends, instead of eating. They should study during the day when they can concentrate better, not at night. Students should also study in a comfortable place while listening to their favourite music. Finally, the students should chew gum. This helps them to relax, and keeps them away from the fridge. If it also helps improve memory, start chewing now!

COMPREHENSION 1   **Decide if the answers to the questions are Yes or No.**

1   Do many people in the USA like to chew gum?

2   Does the American Army like their soldiers to chew gum?

3   Did the group with the imaginary gum have the best results?

4   Do scientists think that chewing gum can help you to concentrate?

5   Do students often study for exams in bad ways?

6   Do scientists think that chewing gum helps students to remember things?

COMPREHENSION 2   **Answer the questions.**

1   In paragraphs 2 and 3, how many reasons are given for chewing gum?

2   In paragraph 4, how many people didn't have any gum?

3   In paragraph 5, how many reasons are given for why chewing gum helps memory?

4   In paragraph 6, how many examples of bad study habits are given?

5   In paragraph 6, how many examples of good study habits are given?

COMPREHENSION 3   **Answer the questions.**

1   In line 1, which phrase means *This is certainly true*?

2   In line 7, which word means *a company that makes things, especially in a factory*?

3   In line 11, what is the opposite of *bad breath*?

4   In line 14, which phrasal verb means *about to happen soon*?

5   In line 18, how many people chewed real gum?

6   In line 30, what does *this* refer to?

   a   more oxygen in the brain

   b   all three groups working at the same speed

7 In lines 32 and 33, what do the study experts give the students?

   a a number of helpful suggestions

   b a collection of sharp points

   c a set of strict rules

8 In line 34, who does *they* refer to?

   a the study experts

   b the students

   c the study experts and the students

9 In lines 39 and 40, which phrase shows that exercise or chatting should replace eating?

10 In lines 43 and 44, what is another way of saying *not go near*?

COMPREHENSION 4 **Complete the sentences that use expressions from the text with the prepositions in the box. Use each preposition only once.**

of   under   up   away   between

1 'Do you have a birthday coming _____?' 'No, it's not for a long time yet.'

2 My father is _____ a lot of stress – he has so much work to do.

3 I'll meet you this afternoon _____ 3.00 and 3.15.

4 My mum says I should read more instead _____ watching TV.

5 Can you keep the dog _____? He's eating my ice cream!

Grammar

Present simple questions

Yes / No questions have short answers.
Is he from Turkey? No, he isn't.
Do you have an exam coming up? Yes, I do.

Wh- questions have short or long answers.
Why is chewing gum so popular? Well, there are many reasons…
Where do you live? Istanbul.

GRAMMAR 1 **Answer the questions about you using short answers.**

1 Are you from Spain?

2 Do you like chewing gum?

3 Does your best friend smoke?

4 Do your friends listen to music a lot?

GRAMMAR 2 **Put the words into their correct order to make *wh-* questions.**

For example:

popular in USA? incredibly is the What

_____*What is incredibly popular in the USA ?*_____

Chewing gum.

1 annual in What USA? the of are gum the sales

_____

$2 billion.

2 gum? Why people chew some do

_____

To have fresh breath.

3 not What gum chewing do? does

_____

It doesn't help you to concentrate.

4 stress? under lot is a of Who

_____

The students who are taking exams.

5 to time a good study? is When

_____

During the day, not at night.

SPEAKING **Talk to a partner and answer the questions.**

1 How do you prepare for exams? Do you exercise during breaks? Do you study until late at night?

2 What are your reasons for chewing gum? If you don't chew gum, what are your reasons for not chewing gum?

3 After chewing gum, where do you put it? Where do most people put their chewing gum when it's finished?

Effective • *Skills*

Label the pictures with a verb.

chew   swallow   spit   bite

swallow

Did you know ? Some countries think spitting in public is very bad. For example, if you spit on the bus you may have to pay a fine.

People in Indiana in the USA are complaining to newspapers about gum-chewing. A journalist asks two of them what the problem is.

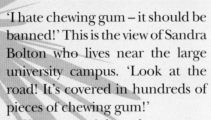

A STICKY PROBLEM

'I hate chewing gum – it should be banned!' This is the view of Sandra Bolton who lives near the large university campus. 'Look at the road! It's covered in hundreds of pieces of chewing gum!'

She was right, there were hundreds of small, black marks all over the road. Who does she blame? 'Young people, especially students, of course. They chew gum all the time and then spit it out on the road. It's disgusting!

I really think we should ban chewing gum like they do in Singapore – that's very sensible. I know for a fact that it costs thousands of dollars to clean the roads.'

It is possible to get a fine if you drop litter, and chewing gum is litter. But, as Mrs Bolton explains, this doesn't happen very much. 'People don't realise how difficult and expensive it is to clean pavements and roads. Chewing gum is almost impossible to remove. It's just bad news.'

Perhaps the best thing then, is to tell people why it's so bad to spit gum on the road. Mrs Bolton disagrees. 'It won't work. Young people just don't care about anything these days.'

Kevin De Souza adds, 'And there are other reasons why gum is so bad. It can be a problem for small animals and birds. They

40 think the gum is food but it can be dangerous: they can die after swallowing gum.'

Mr De Souza also hates finding gum on bus or train seats. 'I once sat on a piece of gum and it was 45 impossible to remove from my trousers. It's always on my shoes, too. The manufacturers make a lot of money from selling gum.

They should pay for cleaning the roads – and my clothes!' 50

The last word is from Mrs Bolton: 'People also look horrible chewing gum with their mouths open. Everything about chewing gum is bad.' 55

What do you think? Should we ban gum – or not?

RESPONDING TO THE TEXT

Decide if the answers to the questions are A or B.

1 What does Mrs Bolton want?

   a She wants a ban on chewing gum.

   b She wants more money to clean the roads.

2 Is chewing gum a problem in other countries, too?

   a Yes

   b No

3 Does Mrs Bolton want to tell people why it's bad to spit gum?

   a Yes

   b No

4 What does Mr De Souza want?

   a He wants the manufacturers to pay for cleaning the roads.

   b He wants more clothes.

IDENTIFYING FACTS AND OPINIONS

Decide if the statements from the text are facts or opinions. Circle F for Fact or O for Opinion.

For example:

Chewing gum should be banned. F /(O)

Sandra Bolton lives near the university campus.(F)/ O

1 The road is covered in hundreds of pieces of chewing gum. F / O

2 Chewing gum is disgusting. F / O

3 It costs a lot of money to clean the roads. F / O

4 Young people don't care about anything these days. F / O

5 The manufacturers make a lot of money from selling gum. F / O

6 People look horrible chewing gum with their mouths open. F / O

VOCABULARY IN CONTEXT Are the words in **bold** countable or uncountable? Fill in the gaps with *is* or *are*.

1 **Gum** _____ a sweet you chew but don't swallow.

2 Some **people** _____ unhappy about the roads.

3 The **news** on TV _____ usually very boring.

4 I think school **food** _____ disgusting.

5 Some **snacks** _____ unhealthy for you.

6 How much **money** _____ in your bag?

SPEAKING Talk to a partner and answer the questions.

1 What's the best way of removing chewing gum from clothes?

2 What do you think of Mrs Bolton? Which of her comments do you agree with?

PRONUNCIATION Find the 10 words in the text. Decide in which words the underlined vowels are pronounced like:

1 /u/ p<u>oo</u>l	2 /ʊ/ g<u>oo</u>d

1 ch<u>e</u>wing ___   5 st<u>u</u>dents ___   9 f<u>oo</u>d ___

2 sh<u>ou</u>ld ___   6 d<u>o</u> ___   10 sh<u>oe</u>s ___

3 l<u>oo</u>k ___   7 rem<u>o</u>ve ___

4 wh<u>o</u> ___   8 n<u>e</u>ws ___

WRITING Write a letter to the newspaper and tell them if you think chewing gum should be banned.

Chewing gum _____ be banned!

I think chewing gum is _____ because

_____.

I also think it's _____.

EXERCISE 1

Read the text.

That's crazy!

Last year Ken went to three foreign countries and had culture shock in each one.

'Japan has the biggest city in the world and guess what? Most of the streets don't have names! I got lost loads of times! My advice is to buy a map before you visit.

In Germany I went to a sauna and I was so shocked! The women and men all sit together – without any clothes on! What a way to make friends!

Then in the UK, some complete strangers called me "love" or "dear". I bought a newspaper in a shop and the assistant said, "There you go, love"! I missed my girlfriend when she said that.'

EXERCISE 2

Match a beginning and an ending to make true sentences about the text.

1	In Japan, he didn't know	a	by what people did together.
2	In Japan, he was shocked	b	strangers were very friendly.
3	In Germany, he was shocked	c	where he was going sometimes.
4	In Germany, he met	d	by what people said to him.
5	In the UK, he was surprised	e	by what towns didn't have.
6	In the UK, he thought that	f	people with no clothes on.

EXERCISE 3

Find the answers in the text. The answers are in this order in the text.

1 Which adjective means *from or in another country?*

2 Which noun means *a feeling of confusion and anxiety that somebody may feel when he or she lives in or visits another country?*

3 Which noun means *a lot of* or *many?*

4 Which noun has a meaning similar to *suggestion?*

5 Which verb means *to spend time with people?*

6 Which verb means *to become a friend of somebody?*

7 Which noun means *people who you do not know?*

8 Which verb means *to feel sad because somebody is not with you anymore?*

EXERCISE 4

Decide in which words the underlined *o* is pronounced like /ɑ/ in *hot*.

1 f<u>o</u>reign

2 sh<u>o</u>ck

3 m<u>o</u>st

4 g<u>o</u>t

5 l<u>o</u>st

6 t<u>o</u>gether

7 cl<u>o</u>thes

8 l<u>o</u>ve

EXERCISE 1

Read the text.

Who was the first Mr Wrigley?

When William Wrigley came to Chicago in 1891, he had just $32. His family were (1) _____ of soap powder and his plan was to promote and sell the soap. The idea was to have a free (2) _____ of gum with every packet. Chewing gum was already for sale but Wrigley decided to add a (3) _____ to make it taste nicer. His idea worked, but the chewing gum was (4) _____ than the packets of soap. So (5) _____ selling soap he decided to sell gum.

Everybody loved the gum: it was cheap, it gave you (6) _____, and it stopped you eating (7) _____. When he died in 1932, Wrigley was one of the ten richest men in America.

EXERCISE 2

Choose a word or phrase to complete the paragraph. Use each word or phrase once only.

fresh breath	instead of	manufacturers
mint flavour	more popular	snacks stick

EXERCISE 3

Decide if the sentences are True (T), False (F), or if the text Doesn't Say (DS).

1 Wrigley was a rich man when he came to Chicago.

T ☐ F ☐ DS ☐

2 He came to Chicago because his family's business was in trouble.

T ☐ F ☐ DS ☐

3 Wrigley sold chewing gum with packets of soap.

T ☐ F ☐ DS ☐

4 He invented chewing gum.

T ☐ F ☐ DS ☐

5 He stopped selling soap and started to sell chewing gum.

T ☐ F ☐ DS ☐

6 There were a lot of different flavours.

T ☐ F ☐ DS ☐

7 When Wrigley died, he was 41 years old.

T ☐ F ☐ DS ☐

8 He was the tenth richest man in America when he died.

T ☐ F ☐ DS ☐

EXERCISE 4

Decide in which words the underlined *ea* is pronounced like /e/ in *bed*.

1 id*ea*

2 alr*ea*dy

3 inst*ea*d

4 ch*ea*p

5 br*ea*th

6 *ea*ting

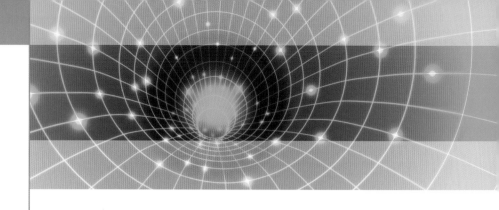

3 • Today's technology

PRE-READING 1 **Solve these anagrams.**

For example:

A *laptop* is a small computer you can carry. (palpot)

1 A _____ is a talk at university given by a professor. (telecur)

2 To _____ is to read your notes and prepare for an exam. (evesir)

3 To _____ is to think very hard while doing something. (accenternot)

4 A _____ is an audio or video file you can record onto your MP3 player or computer. (spatcod)

5 You wear _____ to listen to music on your MP3 player. (anheropes)

6 To _____ is to record something from the Internet onto your MP3 player or computer. (wolddona)

7 A _____ is a place full of books and documents you can look at. (raybirl)

PRE-READING 2 **Put these activities in order of how enjoyable they are from 1 to 9, with 1 as the most enjoyable.**

1 reading books in a library ☐

2 using a computer ☐

3 listening to an MP3 player ☐

4 watching TV ☐

5 studying ☐

6 going to the movies ☐

7 chatting with other students ☐

8 revising ☐

9 using the Internet ☐

Profcasts

Hilary is sitting upstairs in her bedroom surrounded by books and papers for her university courses. Her father knows that Hilary has exams soon and hopes that his daughter is studying hard. But when he goes into her bedroom, what is Hilary doing? Studying? No – she's
5   listening to music on her iPod! Hilary's father is not at all happy until Hilary takes out the earphones and makes her father listen. What can he hear? Music? No – there's a man talking about Pythagoras's theorem, and her father doesn't understand a word of it!

'You see, Dad,' Hilary says, 'I wasn't listening to music – I was
10   studying!' She shows her father the university website which now includes podcasts that students can listen to or watch. She explains that universities in the UK are beginning to see how digital technology can help their students to learn. The days of the lecture and library are not gone, but now it's possible to get information in
15   other ways, too. Her father begins to smile.

Podcasting only started in 2004, but already many websites have audio or video podcasts. You can, of course, keep them on your computer. However, it's also possible to download them onto MP3 players, like Hilary. Then you can listen to or watch them where or
20   whenever you want. That's why they're so popular.

Now university websites also have podcasts (or should we say *profcasts*!). At one British university, for example, a professor records one-hour lectures as podcasts for the university website. Students can then download the lecture onto their MP3 players.

25   How do the students feel about this? Sandra, 19, says: 'Well, in a lecture I listen and take a lot of notes. I can't always follow what the lecturer is saying. But with the podcast I can listen to the lecture many times. Then it's easier for me to understand.' Mark, an
30   engineering student, says 'I usually concentrate more when I'm in a lecture, but it helps me revise.' Not all students are happy, however. David at Leicester University says 'I don't have an MP3
35   player or my own laptop. I use the university computers. Sometimes there are up to 50 other students in the same room, so it can be
40   difficult to concentrate.'

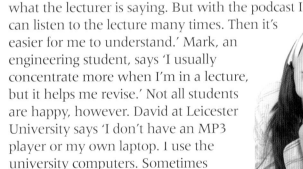

45 What do the lecturers think? Dr Carol Hughes says: 'It's important for universities to use digital technology. Students like using computers, and they like listening to their MP3 players. Now they can study using both.' Professor Jane Webster says: 'Podcasts do not replace normal lectures: they add to them. They give the students extra support. Now it's easier for students to work from home or on the move.' Finally, James Ross adds: 'This is a wonderful thing to have on our website. Students already use the technology to get other news and information, so it seems logical to use it for their studies, too.'

50 Hilary thinks her university's podcasts are great, but her father is in two minds about them. He's glad that Hilary can use her iPod for educational purposes, but then he never knows when she's really studying, or listening to music!

COMPREHENSION 1

Decide which of the sentence endings about the text are true, A or B. Then answer question 3.

1 Universities …

   a … don't want to use digital technology.
   b … think digital technology can help students to learn.

2 University podcasts are popular because …

   a … they are replacing lectures.
   b … you can download them onto MP3 players.

3 Who thinks podcasts of lectures are good?

   a the students
   b the lecturers
   c both

COMPREHENSION 2

Match a student or lecturer (1–6) with their opinion about university podcasts (a–f). Check your answers in the text.

1 Sandra
2 Dr Hughes
3 Mark
4 Professor Webster
5 David
6 Mr Ross

a Podcasts are good for preparing for exams.
b Podcasts help students, they can listen anywhere.
c Digital technology is not new for students.
d Students enjoy using digital technology.
e Podcasts help me to understand the lecture.
f I'm not alone when I listen to podcasts.

COMPREHENSION 3 **Answer the questions.**

1 In line 1, how do we know that Hilary's family doesn't live on one floor?

2 In line 6, which verb means *forces somebody to do something*?

3 In line 20, what does *they* refer to?

   a MP3 players

   b podcasts

   c websites

4 In line 22, what is a *profcast*?

   a a podcast made by a lecturer for students

   b a podcast made by students for their lecturer

   c any podcast made at a university

5 In line 25, another way of saying *What do they think about this?* is _____.

6 In lines 26 and 27, another way of saying *I don't always understand* is _____.

7 In lines 37 and 38, what does *up to 50 other students* mean?

   a 50 students or less

   b more than 50 students

   c exactly 50 students

8 In lines 46 and 47, which phrase means *travelling around*?

9 In lines 50 and 51, which phrase shows that Hilary's father is not sure if university podcasts are a good thing, or not?

COMPREHENSION 4 **Complete the sentences with the verbs in the box.**

> concentrate   follow   include   make   decide   feel

1 My parents _____ me do my homework every evening.

2 How do you _____ about losing the match?

3 It's no good, I can't _____ these instructions at all.

4 I'm in two minds about these jeans. I can't _____ if I like them or not.

5 It's impossible to _____ on my studies with all that noise!

6 University websites have a lot of interesting information; they often _____ podcasts of lectures.

Grammar	Present simple: Routine, habits, facts.
Present simple and present progressive	Hilary **is** a student.

Present simple: Routine, habits, facts.
Hilary **is** a student.
She sits on her bed when she studies.

Present progressive: Actions happening now, descriptions, temporary actions.
Hilary **is sitting** upstairs in her bedroom.
She's studying Maths at university.

GRAMMAR 1   <u>Underline</u> the best verb to complete the sentences.

For example:

At the moment Hilary (listens / <u>is listening</u>) to her iPod.

1   She (listens / is listening) to music everyday.

2   She has exams soon so she (revises / is revising) hard for them.

3   UK universities (begin / are beginning) to use podcasts.

4   Lecutrers often (record / are recording) their lectures as podcasts.

5   Hilary's father (doesn't know / isn't knowing) if he likes the university podcasts.

GRAMMAR 2   **Complete the sentences with the correct form of the verb.**

1   Students usually _____ (study) in the library.

2   Many students _____ (study) in the library now because there are exams soon.

3   Hilary _____ (not travel) far for lectures because her family lives near the university.

4   Her parents _____ (want) her to do well in the exams.

5   So Hilary _____ (try) hard to be the best student in her class!

6   Hilary _____ (think) that getting a good job is important.

SPEAKING   **Talk to a partner and answer the questions.**

1   Where do you like to study? Do you listen to music at the same time? If yes, what music do you listen to?

2   Would you like more of your lectures to be available as podcasts?

3   How do you feel about taking exams?

    a   Fine, I always revise and usually do well.

    b   It depends, sometimes I feel very nervous.

    c   I hate exams, they're awful!

Effective • *Skills*

Label the pictures using the words from the list. Then read a page from a music website.

| speakers | DJ | vinyl record | ~~CD~~ | cassette | record player |

_CD_ _____ _____ _____ _____ _____

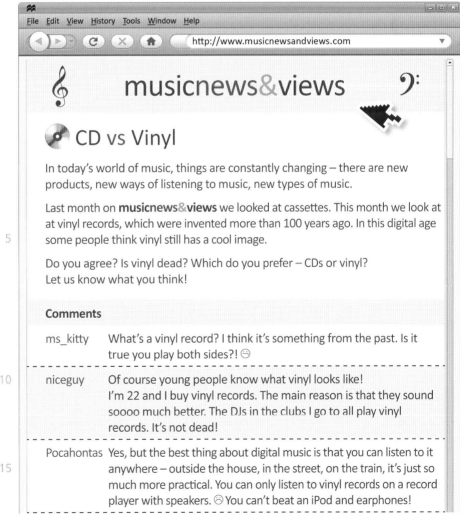

File Edit View History Tools Window Help

http://www.musicnewsandviews.com

musicnews&views

🔵 CD vs Vinyl

In today's world of music, things are constantly changing — there are new products, new ways of listening to music, new types of music.

Last month on **musicnews&views** we looked at cassettes. This month we look at at vinyl records, which were invented more than 100 years ago. In this digital age some people think vinyl still has a cool image.

Do you agree? Is vinyl dead? Which do you prefer — CDs or vinyl?
Let us know what you think!

Comments

ms_kitty	What's a vinyl record? I think it's something from the past. Is it true you play both sides?! ☹
niceguy	Of course young people know what vinyl looks like! I'm 22 and I buy vinyl records. The main reason is that they sound soooo much better. The DJs in the clubs I go to all play vinyl records. It's not dead!
Pocahontas	Yes, but the best thing about digital music is that you can listen to it anywhere — outside the house, in the street, on the train, it's just so much more practical. You can only listen to vinyl records on a record player with speakers. ☹ You can't beat an iPod and earphones!

(line numbers: 5, 10, 15)

20	cool36	It's true! There are usually only about 6 tracks on each side! CDs have more stuff on them, and I can listen to my MP3 for over 15 hours! I also rip CDs onto my computer, so I can listen to them all in one go if I want.
25	niceguy	That's why I buy both CDs and vinyl. I listen to digital music when I'm on the move, I listen to the vinyl records at home. And there are some great designs on the covers, too.
	cool36	Digital music sounds better! Nobody I know buys records – we usually download music from the net. Then we burn them onto CDs or download our favourite tracks straight onto our MP3s. Easy! ☺ ☺
30	Pocahontas	That's great, isn't it? I have a long trip to school so listening to my favourite bands really helps to pass the time! ☺

GENERAL UNDERSTANDING

Decide if the answers to the questions are Yes or No.

1 Were CDs the topic on last month's *Music News & Views*?

2 Is it still possible to buy vinyl records?

3 Can visitors to the website write in with their opinions?

4 Does everyone have the same opinion?

5 Does anybody buy vinyl records?

UNDERSTANDING REFERENCES

Answer the questions with the name of one of the four visitors.

1 Which visitor has never seen a vinyl record?

2 When Pocahontas says, *Yes, but …* who is she replying to?

3 When cool36 says, *It's true*, who is he replying to?

4 Which visitor sees good points in both CDs and vinyl?

5 When cool36 says, *Digital music sounds better*, who is he replying to?

6 Niceguy and which other visitor say they listen to their MP3s when travelling?

VOCABULARY IN CONTEXT | **Find the words or phrases in the text that *Pocahontas* or *cool36* use.**

1 an adjective Pocahontas uses that means *useful* _____

2 a phrase Pocahontas uses that means *this is the best* _____

3 a noun cool36 uses that means *songs, a piece of music* _____

4 a verb cool36 uses that means *record from a CD onto a computer* _____

5 a verb cool36 uses that means *record from a computer onto a CD or MP3 player* _____

6 a noun Pocahontas uses that means *a group of musicians who play together* _____

SPEAKING | **Talk to a partner and answer the questions.**

1 Which visitor's comments do you agree with the most? Why?

2 What is your favourite place to listen to music? Do you prefer listening to music on your own or with friends?

3 What's your favourite band?

PRONUNCIATION 1 | **Decide in which words the underlined _ea_ is pronounced like /i/ in r_ea_ding?**

1 r_ea_son	3 sp_ea_kers	5 _ea_rphones
2 d_ea_d	4 b_ea_t	6 gr_ea_t

PRONUNCIATION 2 | **Find the seven nouns in the text. Decide if the first or second syllable is stressed.**

1 music	(●●)/●●	5 product	●●/●●
2 cassettes	●●/●●	6 earphones	●●/●●
3 records	●●/●●	7 designs	●●/●●
4 vinyl	●●/●●		

WRITING | **Add your own comment to the *Music News & Views* website.**

I prefer to buy _____ .

I think _____ are better than _____

because _____ .

Also _____ .

4 • Urban life

Match the words to make a phrase.

1	get up	**a**	with friends
2	live in	**b**	animals
3	feed	**c**	early
4	meet up	**d**	a flat

Now do the same with these.

5	make	**e**	to university
6	go	**f**	fruit
7	listen	**g**	a decision
8	pick	**h**	to music

Which of these activities do you think are done in the country, in the city, or both? Tick (✔) the box.

		country	city	both
1	get up late			
2	have breakfast with the family			
3	have lunch outside			
4	chat on the phone			
5	go to a cinema			
6	drive a tractor			
7	have coffee in a shopping centre			
8	have a boring Sunday			

Read and check your answers.

Worlds apart

Because their fathers are brothers, American teenagers Ronald and Jessica are cousins. A generation ago, one brother decided to stay in the country while the other chose to move to the city. Both cousins go to school, and this September both will go to college, but at the
5   moment their day-to-day lives are worlds apart.

Ronald lives with his family in a house in the country in California, and here he describes a typical weekend.

'Saturday mornings are the same as any mornings. I always get up early and feed the animals. I also drop by the farm next door to get
10   some fresh milk. Our family always has a big breakfast together that my mom cooks, usually with our own eggs and homemade bread.

Then, without fail, we all go off to the market where we swap our vegetables for other things we need. The market is a weekly meeting for all the local families, and in the evening there's often a barbecue
15   somewhere.

What we do on Sundays depends on the time of year. After breakfast, dad and I often spend the morning cutting wood or picking fruit. We might plant some vegetables or mend some machinery, and I sometimes drive the tractor. Then after lunch, which is nearly always
20   sandwiches and fruit that we have outside, the afternoon is free to do what I want. If I have any school exams or homework I study in the treehouse. I always go there when I want to be alone; I often listen to my MP3 player or chat on the phone. Sometimes some of the other local boys and I take a hike in the woods. If it's really hot we swim in
25   the river – but the water's always freezing! In the evening we might play pool at the local club, or watch a DVD at someone's home. I'm usually in bed by 10 pm as I'm up early again before I go to school.'

Jessica, on the other hand, lives with her family in an apartment on a busy Los Angeles city street. This is her typical weekend.

30   'Saturdays are my favourite day of the week because I always meet up with friends and go shopping. I usually skip breakfast. I just get up and go straight out. We meet at the bus stand and it's a 30-minute journey downtown if there's not too much traffic. Then we go and have a coffee in the shopping mall. Most of the day is spent just wandering
35   around and buying clothes and music. Lunch is usually in a fast-food

40

restaurant, where we eat burgers and milkshakes or pizza and cola. Saturday evenings are either spent at a disco, at a movie theatre, or going bowling – something like that. I never stay in.

Sundays can be boring. I get up very late, sometimes in the afternoon, and make myself a sandwich. I usually stay in my room most of the day studying and listening to music, or chatting on the phone to my friends. We often meet up again in the evening in a café. I usually get home quite late, so it's possible that I don't see my parents all weekend!'

COMPREHENSION 1 **Answer the questions about the two cousins.**

1 Which cousin spends a lot of money?

    a Ronald   **b** Jessica   **c** both

2 Which cousin spends a lot of time with their family?

    a Ronald   **b** Jessica   **c** both

3 Which cousin studies on a Sunday?

    a Ronald   **b** Jessica   **c** both

4 Which cousin spends time alone at the weekend?

    a Ronald   **b** Jessica   **c** both

5 Which cousin has a weekend that changes during the year?

    a Ronald   **b** Jessica   **c** both

COMPREHENSION 2 **Answer the questions.**

1 In lines 2 and 3, when did one brother decide to move to the city?

    a last year

    b when he was about the same age as his children are now

    c when he was a small boy

2 In line 5, which phrase shows that Ronald and Jessica live very different lives?

3 In line 9, how long does Ronald stay at the farm next door?

    a He spends some time there milking the cows.

    b He spends all morning there.

    c He goes there for a short time.

4   In line 12, a phrase that shows that something *happens all the time* is _____?

5   In lines 12 and 13, what does the family do with the vegetables at the market?

   a   They sell them.

   b   They exchange them for something else.

   c   They give them away.

6   In line 24, another way of saying a *long walk in the country* is _____?

7   In line 28, which phrase shows that there is a contrast between Jessica's and Ronald's lives?

8   In line 31, which sentence is correct?

   a   Jessica doesn't usually have breakfast.

   b   Jessica usually jumps up and down while she has breakfast.

   c   Jessica never has breakfast.

9   In lines 34 and 35, another way of saying *walking slowly without a particular purpose or direction* is _____?

10   In lines 37 and 38, what does Jessica do on a Saturday night?

   a   She stays in.

   b   She goes out.

   c   She visits her friends.

COMRPEHENSION 3   **Complete the sentences about the text with the prepositions in the box. Use each preposition only once.**

at   through   with   off   around   on   up   out

1   Ronald lives _____ his family in a big house

2   Ronald's family all go _____ to the market together.

3   He likes chatting _____ the phone with his friends.

4   In the summer, he walks _____ the woods.

5   Sometimes there's a game of pool _____ the local club.

6   Jessica skips breakfast and goes straight _____.

7   She enjoys walking _____ the shopping centre.

8   Sometimes she meets _____ with her friends again later.

Grammar	*always:* in all situations I **always** get up early.	*sometimes:* what happens in some situations I **sometimes** drive the tractor.
Adverbs of frequency	*usually:* what happens in most situations I'm **usually** in bed by 10 pm.	*never:* at no time, not at all I **never** stay in.
	often: what happens in many situations Dad and I **often** spend the morning picking fruit.	

GRAMMAR 1   <u>Underline</u> the best adverb to make true sentences about Ronald or Jessica.

1   Ronald's family (always / usually) has eggs for breakfast.

2   They (always / sometimes) go to the Saturday market.

3   Ronald (sometimes / usually) has sandwiches for lunch.

4   Ronald (usually / sometimes) swims in the river.

5   He (often / never) plays pool on a Saturday night.

6   Jessica's bus (sometimes / usually) takes 30 minutes to get into town.

7   She (always / often) goes out on a Saturday night.

8   She (often / sometimes) sees her parents at the weekend.

GRAMMAR 2   Complete the sentences with information about you.

1   At the weekend I always …

2   With my friends I sometimes …

3   With my parents I never …

4   At school I often …

5   In the evening I usually …

6   In the morning I always …

With my parents I never …

SPEAKING   Talk to a partner and answer the questions.

1   Are your weekends more like Ronald's or Jessica's? How?

2   Which cousin has the more interesting weekend? Why?

3   Which cousin would have a bigger problem: Ronald moving to the city, or Jessica moving to the country? Can you explain why?

Effective • *Skills*

Read the text quickly to find these words in bold and complete the sentences.

| rural   populated   available   overcrowded   urban |

1 We can't eat here now because there are no tables _____.

2 I want to live in the city because I prefer an _____ lifestyle.

3 If you like the country it's better to live in a _____ area.

4 I hate the train in the mornings when there are too many people: it's so _____.

5 With 19 million people, New York is America's most _____ city.

Living in the City

Jessica's father moved to the city because he wanted a better job.

'I know I did the right thing,' he says. 'I have a good job and earn a lot of money. I also know that the education Jessica has here is better than in the country. She's going to university this autumn. The healthcare facilities are also good – the main hospital is just a few blocks away if there's an emergency. The sports facilities are excellent, too. I usually play squash and swim twice a week. My wife and I sometimes go to the theatre in the evening, or see an exhibition.

On the other hand, it's also an expensive place to live. We can't live in a large house like Ronald's family. Jessica has a lot of fun though. Often we don't see her at the weekend, but I'm happy because there's lots for her to do. She has many choices – where to shop, what to eat, who her friends are – that are not **available** in the country. I think Ronald's life is more boring.'

Jessica's father is not alone in coming to the city for work. Many people come looking for a job; others come to study and then stay. In 2006, according to the United Nations, about the same number of people worldwide lived in the country and in the city. Now more people live in the city.

20 Africa has the highest rate of urban growth, but Asia has more people living in urban areas. Six out of the ten biggest cities in the world are in Asia. In 2015, Asia will have more people living in cities than the rest of the world put together. For example, the USA has about 40 cities of more than a million people, but China has over 100. Japan is

25 one of the world's most densely populated nations, with a minority of people living in rural areas.

What is the result of this urban growth? It's overcrowded cities with little fresh air, lots of noise and more pollution. On the other hand, cities offer greater choice, higher salaries, and more cultural activities.

30 Jessica and her family prefer the city. Do you prefer it too?

GENERAL UNDERSTANDING

Decide if the sentences are True (T) or False (F).

1 Jessica's father wants to live in a large house in the country.   T ☐   F ☐

2 He thinks Jessica's life is more interesting than her cousin's.   T ☐   F ☐

3 More then 50 per cent of the world's population live in the country.   T ☐   F ☐

4 Africa has the fastest growing cities in the world.   T ☐   F ☐

5 More than three quarters of Japanese people live in urban areas.   T ☐   F ☐

6 There are good things and bad things about living in the city.   T ☐   F ☐

VOCABULARY IN CONTEXT

Find two words or phrases in the text that are related to the words in the left column.

For example:

work   ____*good job; earn money*____

1 healthcare   _____

2 education   _____

3 sports   _____

4 culture   _____

5 continents   _____

READING FOR DETAIL Match a beginning (1–6) and an ending (a–f) to make true sentences about the text.

1 Jessica's father

2 Jessica's parents

3 Jessica

4 Ronald's family

5 Asia

6 China

a live in a large house.

b has more than 100 million people living in cities.

c has the biggest cities in the world.

d like going to see plays in the evening.

e is going to university after the summer.

f plays sports a couple of times a week.

SPEAKING Talk to a partner and answer the questions.

1 Do you prefer living in the city or the country? Why?

2 In what ways can living in the city be bad for you?

3 Is it better for poor people to live in the city or the country? Why?

PRONUNCIATION Find the 12 words in the text. Decide in which words the underlined a is pronounced like:

1 /æ/ h<u>a</u>ve	2 /eɪ/ pl<u>a</u>y	3 /ə/ hospit<u>a</u>l	4 /e/ <u>a</u>ny

1 s<u>a</u>ys	4	5 r<u>a</u>te	___	9 Chin<u>a</u>	___
2 h<u>a</u>nd	___	6 <u>A</u>sia	___	10 Jap<u>a</u>n	___
3 m<u>a</u>ny	___	7 urb<u>a</u>n	___	11 n<u>a</u>tion	___
4 <u>A</u>frica	___	8 <u>a</u>rea	___	12 rur<u>a</u>l	___

Which group does Afric<u>a</u> ___ and J<u>a</u>pan ___ belong to?

WRITING Where do you prefer *not* to live – in the country or in the city? Explain why you don't want to live there.

I prefer not to live in the ... because ... .

I also think the ... is better than the ... because ... .

EXERCISE 1

Read the text.

MP3 Profs

Not everyone is happy about the increasing use of online teaching at universities. Professor Jim Bartlett says the traditional classroom is still more important.

'I'm in two minds about how good university podcasts really are. I know that if students can't follow what was said in a lecture, they can download it from our website and listen again. However, I think it can stop students concentrating when they listen the first time. Also, the relationship between a lecturer and students cannot be replaced. In the digital world, students can't ask questions. Those who walk around between classes wearing earphones don't hear what's going on around them.'

EXERCISE 2

Decide if the sentences are True (T), False (F), or if the text Doesn't Say (DS).

1 More and more universities are using podcasts.

   T ☐ F ☐ DS ☐

2 Professor Bartlett is totally negative about university podcasts.

   T ☐ F ☐ DS ☐

3 The professor thinks that podcasts may make students lazy.

   T ☐ F ☐ DS ☐

4 He believes that students should be able to ask questions.

   T ☐ F ☐ DS ☐

5 He says that listening to MP3 players is bad for the ears.

   T ☐ F ☐ DS ☐

6 Students listen to music in the classrooms.

   T ☐ F ☐ DS ☐

EXERCISE 3

Complete the sentences with the words in the box.

rip   speakers   burn   download
track   digital

1 I love all the songs on this CD, but my favourite _____ is the last one.

2 Students can _____ the lectures from the university website and listen to them on their MP3 players or computers.

3 If you're worried about your computer getting a virus, you should _____ your work on a CD so you don't lose it.

4 Which do you like better – _____ music or vinyl?

5 I prefer listening to music on my laptop when I work, so I usually _____ CDs onto the computer.

6 I can't hear very well. I was standing too close to the _____ at the concert last night.

EXERCISE 1

Read the text.

The good life

Ronald's father decided to stay in the country because he wanted a better life for his family.

'I understand why my brother **moved**,' he says. 'For me, however, a safe family life is more important than money. Cities are often **dangerous** places to live in, and unhealthy, too. They're usually **overcrowded**, with not much fresh air and a lot of **pollution**. Ronald eats well (he'd never **skip** breakfast like Jessica does!), and he doesn't **wander around** with nothing to do. He's going to university soon, which shows that the **local** school is good. I just hope he decides to return here after his studies, so that future **generations** can live the good life, too.'

EXERCISE 2

Choose the correct word to make true sentences about the text.

1 Ronald's father wanted a better life *so* / *because* he stayed in the country.

2 Ronald's father stayed in the country *but* / *so* he understands why his brother left.

3 Ronald's father thinks that *many* / *a few* cities are dangerous.

4 He also thinks that *all* / *most* cities have little fresh air.

5 Ronald *always* / *never* has breakfast.

6 Ronald is *never* / *usually* busy.

7 Ronald is going to college *although* / *so* his school isn't bad.

8 Ronald's father hopes his grandchildren *also* / *don't* live in the country.

EXERCISE 3

Complete the sentences with a word or phrase in **bold** from the text.

1 The shops in our neighbourhood are good, especially the _____ supermarket.

2 Our family has lived here for a few _____, from my great grandparents' time.

3 Prisoners and staff are unhappy because the jails are _____.

4 There aren't so many fish here because of _____ in the river.

5 This city is safe during the day, but it's _____ at night.

6 Let's _____ the last class and go shopping instead!

7 Yes, we can _____ the shopping centre and maybe meet up with some friends.

8 My family _____ to the UK when my dad got a job in London.

5 Getting away

PRE-READING 1   **Match an activity with a country.**

1	Riding across the desert on a camel	**a**	South America
2	Scuba diving off the Great Barrier Reef	**b**	Jordan
3	Visiting a game park	**c**	Australia
4	Walking through the rainforest	**d**	Switzerland
5	Speaking three languages	**e**	South Africa
6	Working in a refugee camp	**f**	Morocco

PRE-READING 2   **Answer the questions before reading about young British people who decide to travel overseas before starting university.**

1   What is a *consultant*?

    a   a government official

    b   an expert whose job is to give help and advice on a particular subject

    c   the title given to Muslim rulers in some countries

2   What is a *retired* person?

    a   a person who has stopped working because of their age

    b   a person who has worked very hard and needs a rest

    c   a woman who has just had a baby

3   What is a *volunteer*?

    a   a person who is made to do a job they don't want to do

    b   a person who does a job and gets paid for it

    c   a person who does a job but does not get paid for it

4   What is an *instructor*?

    a   a person who builds things, like cars

    b   a person whose job is to teach people a practical skill or sport

    c   a person whose job is to check that things are working correctly

Take a trip

Travel across South America and explore the rainforest! Teach English in a village in Ghana! Run a game park in South Africa! Work in a refugee camp in Jordan!

A holiday brochure? A travel agent's advertisement? Not exactly. These are just a few of the thousands of activities that people can choose to do during their gap year. It's a growing market – but what is a gap year and why do so many people take one?

Naomi Sherwood, a gap year consultant, explains: 'A gap year is a period of time, not always a full year, between one stage of your life and another. For some it's a few weeks, for others, six months or longer. It can be anytime, perhaps during a career change or just after retiring. However, the most popular gap year is after school and before university. What someone does during that time is up to them, and for young people nowadays the choice is enormous. It's sometimes difficult for them to know what to do.'

That's why Ms Sherwood helps people choose the best option.

'I get the students to consider doing something that's important to them,' she says. 'Do they like travelling and meeting people? Do they want to do something that will help them with their university studies? Do they want to be useful? Do they want to learn a foreign language? Do they need to get a job to help pay for their studies, or get work experience?'

Ms Sherwood has helped many people make the most of their gap year. For Peter, very keen on sports and languages, it was an easy decision. He went to a town in the Alps where he worked as a ski instructor and improved his French, German and Italian. He loved being away from his parents and England. He returned home a happier and more mature person.

Rachel was interested in finding out about a completely different culture, and she also wanted to help people. She decided to work as a volunteer in a refugee camp in Jordan. For her, the experience was incredible, and it helped her to become more independent and more confident. Going to university after that was a lot easier for her.

Dan says he now has a better understanding of the world. He met a lot of new people and had many new experiences while working in a hospital in Zimbabwe. He went there after one year at medical school in London. He found that health conditions were far worse than in the UK so it was a challenging year, but very rewarding, too. He returned to his studies more motivated and even keener to become a doctor.

40 | Anna spent half her gap year trekking through Argentina and Chile. However, because she wants to be a vet, she also worked for four months with monkeys in an animal refuge in Bolivia. She had an amazing time and worked very hard. She was up at 7.30 every day and worked until 6pm, but she loved it.

45 | Ms Sherwood says, 'Whatever people decide to do, they usually come back more confident, happier and better prepared for life at university.'

COMPREHENSION 1 **Decide if the answers to the questions are *Yes* or *No*.**

1 Do only young people take a gap year?

2 Is Naomi Sherwood a student?

3 Can Peter speak four languages?

4 Did Rachel get paid for her work?

5 Did Dan go to Zimbabwe before he started his studies?

6 Did all the 'gappers' have a good experience?

COMPREHENSION 2 **Try to answer these questions about the two readings.**

1 In line 6, which sentence is correct?

   a Fewer and fewer people are taking a gap year.

   b More and more people are taking a gap year.

   c The same amount of people are taking a gap year.

2 In lines 8 to 13, which sentence is correct?

   a A gap year can be less than a year and can be taken at any time.

   b A gap year is always a full year and can be taken at any time.

   c A gap year is always taken between school and university.

3 In lines 13 to 14, what phrase shows that the students can decide what to do?

4 In line 18, who does *them* refer to?

   a the universities

   b the parents

   c the students

5 In lines 18 to 22, who answers the questions?

   a Naomi Sherwood.

   b The people who want to take a gap year.

   c The travel agents.

6 In line 23, which phrase means *to gain as much advantage or enjoyment as possible*?

7 In line 28, which phrase means *more sensible and grown up*?

8 In line 33, another way of saying *certain about your abilities and not nervous or frightened* is _____.

9 In line 38, another way of saying *difficult in an interesting way* is _____.

10 In line 45, what does *it* refer to?

   a trekking through Argentina and Chile

   b working with monkeys

   c working on holidays

COMPREHENSION 3   **Complete the sentences with the adjectives in the box. Use each adjective only once.**

> enormous   fluent   independent   rewarding   motivated   amazing

1 Tim is happy being a teacher and thinks it's a _____ career.

2 The Great Pyramid of Giza is _____, it's over 140 metres tall.

3 Janet is an _____ student, she likes working on her own.

4 Rui is a _____ student, he's very interested in his studies and works hard.

5 Rima can speak French very well, I think she's _____.

6 Ahmed lived without electricity for six months. That's _____!

COMPREHENSION 4   **Complete the sentences with a linking word from the box. Use each word only once.**

> and   because   although   but   however   so

1 _____ a gap year can be any time, the most popular time to take one is before university.

2 Ms Sherwood helps the students _____ it's difficult for them to know what to do.

3 Peter wanted to ski _____ practise his languages.

4 Rachel wanted to take a gap year _____ she didn't want just a holiday.

5 Working in Zimbabwe was difficult for Dan. _____, it made him more interested in medicine.

6 Anna wants to be a vet _____ she worked with animals.

Grammar	Adjectives with one syllable:
Comparative adjectives	*Dan was **keener** to become a doctor.*

Adjectives ending in –*y*:
*Rachel was **happier** after her gap year.*

Adjectives with two or more syllables:
*People became **more confident**.*

Irregular adjectives:
*He now has a **better** understanding of the world.*
*The health conditions were far **worse**.*

GRAMMAR 1 **Complete the sentences with the adjectives in the box. Make the adjective comparative.**

> popular   easy   new   interested   bad   good

1 After a year in Spain it was _____ for me to speak Spanish.

2 I only spoke in English, so my Arabic is _____ now than before!

3 A gap year before university is _____ than after university.

4 Roy thinks it's _____ to help people than just have a holiday.

5 Now I'm _____ in people from other cultures than before.

6 Dan uses _____ medical techniques and more modern equipment in London.

GRAMMAR 2 **Complete the sentences with comparative adjectives to make true sentences about you.**

1 I'm now _____ than two years ago.

2 English is _____ than the other subjects I study.

3 When my parents were young, they were _____ than me.

4 After graduating my life will be _____.

SPEAKING **Talk to a partner and answer the questions.**

1 Do people in your country take a gap year? If so, what kind of things do they do?

2 How do you feel about students taking a gap year?

   a It's a great idea!

   b I think it's better to go straight to university.

   c It's for young people who have too much time and money.

3 Which things may be more difficult for people when they come back home?

Effective • *Skills*

SKIMMING AND
SCANNING **Quickly read an interview with a professor who dislikes gap years. Match a question (a-e) with each of his replies.**

    a It can be expensive, can't it?

    b Don't some people come back more mature and more interested in their studies?

    c ~~Why do you think it's a waste of time?~~

    d What about the people who work and save money for the trip?

    e But some people work, for example by teaching English. Isn't that good?

MIND THE GAP

1 Not everyone thinks the gap year is a good idea. Professor Vince Barkham thinks it's all a 'waste of time'.

    1   *Why do you think it's a waste of time?*

'The main reason is because I think for most people it's just a long holiday. They spend their time on the beach and having a party. It doesn't help them
5 with their studies and it doesn't help them to get a job either. They often don't get to know the local people; they spend their time with other British people.'

    2 _____

'No, not really. It's much better to teach English after you are trained to be an English teacher. Just because you speak a language doesn't mean that
10 you are good at teaching it. An 18-year-old is not skilled enough to do a good job. It's just playing at work.'

    3 _____

'Yes, and that's another reason I'm against the idea. The students who have rich parents go away with their father's credit card. They can spend what they like. This doesn't help them to understand money; it's just a free
15 holiday.'

4 _____

'I agree there are some people who pay for the trip themselves. However, it's better to use this money to pay for university, which is very expensive, than to spend it on an adventure in Nepal.'

20

5 _____

'Some, yes. But many of them are less motivated now. They're bored and want to start travelling again. Also for the students who didn't have a gap year, they have to listen to all the boring stories again and again!'

GENERAL UNDERSTANDING

Decide if the sentences about Professor Barkham are True (T) or False (F).

1 Professor Barkham thinks gap year people usually make friends with foreigners.   T ☐   F ☐

2 He thinks that people shouldn't teach English during their gap years.   T ☐   F ☐

3 He says people from rich families don't learn about money.   T ☐   F ☐

4 He thinks it's OK to spend money on a gap year if people have worked for it beforehand.   T ☐   F ☐

5 He says there is a difference between those who have had a gap year, and those who haven't.   T ☐   F ☐

6 He is negative about the gap year and about British students, too.   T ☐   F ☐

READING FOR DETAIL

Match an *adjective* in column A with a *noun* in column B to a *phrase* in column C.

A	B	C
1 long	parents	get everything they want
2 English	fees	are what you pay to go to university
3 rich	holiday	are repeated all the time
4 expensive	students	which doesn't help their studies
5 British	stories	need to be trained
6 boring	teachers	pay for their kid's gap year

VOCABULARY IN CONTEXT

Notice the difference between the two adjectives *bored* and *boring* in the reading:

Students are bored and want to travel again.

They have to listen to all the boring stories again.

Decide whether the following adjectives should have *–ing* or *–ed* endings.

1   I think travelling round South America is a *fascinating / fascinated* thing to do.

2   Are your parents *retiring / retired*, or are they still working?

3   'The Niagra Falls are incredible!' 'Yes, they're *amazing / amazed*.'

4   I'm so *disappointing / disappointed* I didn't take a gap year.

5   Now I'm more *motivating / motivated* to work harder at university.

6   Working in a refugee camp was very *rewarding / rewarded*.

SPEAKING   **Talk to a partner and answer the questions.**

1   Do you agree that a gap year is a waste of time? Why? / Why not?

2   Do you think that in general it's easier to be a student now than in the past?

3   Imagine you have six months off next year. Where do you want to go, and what do you want to do there?

WRITING   **Your university wants to know what students think about taking a gap year. Answer the question and then add a few lines to explain your opinion.**

I think taking a gap year before university is …

☐ a good thing   ☐ a bad thing

I think that taking a gap year is … because … .

I think it's very important / not important to work for

a while because … .

I also think … .

6 • The piracy business

PRE-READING 1 **Match the words to the correct picture: A or B.**

cheap	real	pirated	fake	genuine	market
copy	designer label		shop	counterfeit	expensive

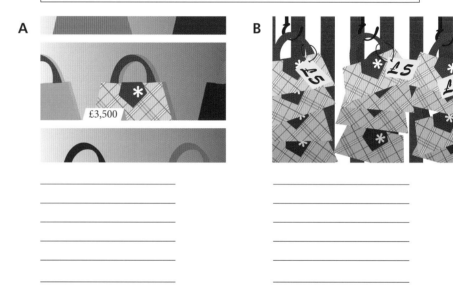

A

£3,500

B

_____   _____

_____   _____

_____   _____

_____   _____

_____   _____

_____   _____

PRE-READING 2 **Complete the sentences with the words in the box.**

counterfeit (adj)	pirated (adj)	fake (n)
designer labels (n)	genuine (adj)	piracy (n)

1 This perfume smells nice, but it's very cheap. I don't think it's
_____.

2 My father has a Rolex watch, but it never tells the right time, so I
know it's a _____.

3 I never buy expensive computer programmes. I only download
_____ software from the Internet.

4   That market sells many _____ goods very cheaply.

5   Police in the UK say that the _____ business is 'seen as normal' by most people.

6   My sister likes to wear expensive, fashionable clothes, so she buys only _____.

Big labels small prices

Diane is a student at a university far away from her home town. Now it's the end of term and she's buying presents to take home for her family. For her mum, she buys a Chanel handbag and a bottle of French perfume. For her brother, she buys an Adidas sports shirt and
5   some music CDs. For her sister, she buys a Gucci bag and some DVDs. She hasn't made up her mind what to buy for her dad yet – perhaps a Rolex watch.

Is she rich? No, not at all. So how can Diane buy all these things for her family? The answer is simple – none of the things are genuine.
10   She doesn't buy any of these things from a shop. Some things come from the market and some things from street traders. They are all fakes. They are all counterfeit goods.

Perhaps this may seem normal to you. Perhaps you too buy counterfeit goods. It's one way of buying 'designer label' clothes. It's
15   also a way of buying music and films without spending a lot of money. Sometimes it's very difficult to tell the difference between the real thing and a copy. If you can buy counterfeit goods cheaply, that's not a bad thing, is it? Does it matter?

Many companies are very worried, for two reasons. Firstly, the
20   companies lose money. In Europe, about 11 per cent of clothing and footwear, and 12 per cent of toys and sportswear, may be counterfeit. In China, most films and software are believed to be fakes. Billions of dollars are lost every year from people buying counterfeit goods and downloading pirated games and software from the Internet. This
25   means less money to develop new goods and prevent viruses. Asian software developers working for small businesses struggle to survive.

Secondly, fake goods are not as safe as genuine goods. One reason why fake goods are much cheaper is that no money is spent on checking safety. Another reason is that the goods are often made
30   with poor-quality materials. Toys are a good example. Children like to put their toys in their mouth. If the toys have sharp parts, or are covered in a paint that is not safe, this can be a serious problem.

35 Another example is car parts. If the brakes are not genuine, the car may not stop in an emergency. Mothers who buy counterfeit toys cannot be sure that the toys are safe for their children. Drivers who buy fake car parts cannot be sure that their car is safe to drive. If there's a problem, there's no customer support – and you certainly won't get your money back.

40 Buying counterfeit goods means two things. You take money away from companies that make safe goods and you give money to counterfeiters who don't care about safety. Next time you buy a cheap designer label or download pirated software, think about where your money goes. If the product breaks, has a virus, or is unsafe, the only person you can blame is yourself.

COMPREHENSION 1   **Decide if the sentences about the text are True (T) or False (F).**

1 Diana has a lot of money.   T ☐   F ☐

2 All the things that Diana buys are counterfeit.   T ☐   F ☐

3 Counterfeit goods never look the same as the real thing.   T ☐   F ☐

4 There are two reasons why companies are worried.   T ☐   F ☐

5 Some counterfeit goods can be dangerous.   T ☐   F ☐

6 The author thinks that buying counterfeit goods is a
   bad thing.   T ☐   F ☐

COMPREHENSION 2   **Answer the questions.**

1 In line 6, what is another way of saying *She hasn't decided*?

2 In lines 11 and 12, what does *They* refer to?

   a things for sale on the street
   b the things that Diane buys for her family
   c things for sale in the market

3 In line 13, what does *this* refer to?

   a buying counterfeit goods
   b buying things from a market
   c buying things on the street

4 In line 18, what is the meaning of *Does it matter*?

   a Is buying fake goods something important to think about?
   b Is buying fake goods a bad thing to do?

5 In line 30, what are toys a good example of?

   a fake goods that are not as safe as genuine goods

   b fake goods that are cheaper than genuine goods

6 In line 31, what adjective means *something that can cut you*?

7 In lines 33 and 34, what problem can fake brakes cause?

   a The car may stop too quickly.

   b The car may have problems starting.

   c The car may have problems stopping if there is a sudden and dangerous situation.

8 In line 37, which phrase means *help from the people who sell the goods*?

9 In lines 37 and 38, what does *get your money back* mean?

   a have your money returned

   b lose a lot of money

   c make a lot of money

10 In line 44, what is another way of saying *You are the person who made the problem. No one else is responsible*?

COMPREHENSION 3 **Match the words to make a phrase. Read again to check your answers.**

1	To spend	**a**	pirated software
2	To tell	**b**	money
3	To download	**c**	viruses
4	To develop	**d**	to survive
5	To prevent	**e**	the difference
6	To struggle	**f**	new goods

Complete the sentences with a phrase from above.

1 On holiday it's nice _____ on yourself.

2 My brother likes _____, especially computer games.

3 'Is this tea or coffee?' 'With that colour it's difficult _____!'

4 Most companies want _____ and get more customers.

5 I hope your computer has a programme _____.

6 In today's business world you have _____.

Grammar	*If you buy counterfeit goods,*
Conditional sentences	*… you **can** save money.* (This is something you are able to do) *… or… you **might** save money.* (This is possible, but it depends) *… or… you **will** save money.* (This is definite)

GRAMMAR 1 **Match the beginning of a sentence (1–6) with an ending (a–f) to make sentences about the text.**

1 If you buy cheap goods,   a the stall owner will laugh.

2 If the toys are not genuine,   b you can easily get a virus.

3 If the brakes are not real,   c you can't go to the police.

4 If the software is fake,   d they might be fake.

5 If you ask for your money back,   e the car might not stop.

6 If you have a serious problem,   f children might get hurt.

GRAMMAR 2 **What do you think *can*, *might*, or *will* happen in these situations? Complete the sentences with your opinion.**

1 If I only buy fake goods, _____.

2 If it's difficult to tell the difference between fake and genuine goods, _____.

3 If I don't study very hard, _____.

4 If my English gets better, _____.

SPEAKING **Talk to a partner and answer the questions.**

1 Do you, or people you know, sometimes buy counterfeit clothes? If yes, give some examples.

2 Do you often download pirated software, music, or films? If yes, give some examples.

3 The text describes the problems with fake toys and fake car parts. What problems do you think there may be with fake drinks, fake medicine, or fake mobile phones?

Effective • *Skills*

PRE-READING **Tick (✔) the way you get your music. You can tick more than one box.**

I buy CDs from music shops. ☐

I buy pirated CDs. ☐

I borrow CDs from friends and copy them. ☐

I buy music from the Internet, for example through iTunes. ☐

I download free music from illegal websites. ☐

I download free music. I don't know if this is legal or not. ☐

I download music from my friends' websites. ☐

Compare your answers with another student's.

Digital Downloads

There was a time when buying music meant only one thing – you went into a shop and paid for it. You can still buy it from a shop, of course, but you can also buy it from the Internet. However, nowadays, you don't even need to buy music – you can just download it for free. For many people,
5 the last option is the simplest and quickest, and costs nothing – but it's not always legal.

Jammie Thomas, a woman from Minnesota in the USA, downloaded and shared thousands of music files over the Internet. Unfortunately for her, the music companies were not happy. She became the first case to go to
10 court, and she had to pay a fine of $222,000 to six different music companies. They said she had acted illegally because she didn't have the copyright to share the music. The companies hoped that this large fine would clearly demonstrate that downloading music from illegal sites is unacceptable.

15 Ms Thomas isn't alone in having downloaded music from the Internet for free. Billions of songs are downloaded each year, but only one in 20 is paid for. The music companies are angry with people sharing music files because it means they get no money for them, and neither do the artists who make the music. In 2007, British band *Radiohead* decided to do

20 something different. They decided to sell their seventh album over the Internet as a digital download. This decision was important for two reasons. Firstly, the band sold the album through their own website; they didn't use a record company. Secondly, the band said that buyers could decide how much they wanted to spend. They could spend as little or as
25 much as they liked. Perhaps not surprisingly, most people chose not to pay anything! However, worldwide, 38 per cent did pay for the album, and they paid an average of $6 each. 1.2 million people visited the site. So, if a million people downloaded the music, then *Radiohead* received $2,280,000. Musicians usually only receive a small amount of money from
30 the price of a CD. *Radiohead* received all the money; nothing was spent on packaging, and no money was paid to the music company, of course.

Digital downloading is changing the music business. Will music companies become a thing of the past?

GENERAL UNDERSTANDING

Decide if the sentences about the text are True (T) or False (F).

1 It's illegal to download music from the Internet without paying for it. T ☐ F ☐

2 Jammie Thomas was the first person to pay a big fine. T ☐ F ☐

3 Only a few people download and share music illegally. T ☐ F ☐

4 *Radiohead* don't have a music company. T ☐ F ☐

5 Many people got a *Radiohead* album for nothing. T ☐ F ☐

6 *Radiohead* now sell their albums on YouTube. T ☐ F ☐

SCANNING

Decide if the answers are Yes (Y), No (N), or if the text Doesn't Say (DS).

1 Is Jammie Thomas American? Y ☐ N ☐ DS ☐

2 Is she married? Y ☐ N ☐ DS ☐

3 Was her fine almost a quarter of a million dollars? Y ☐ N ☐ DS ☐

4 Have *Radiohead* made more than six albums? Y ☐ N ☐ DS ☐

5 Was the *Radiohead* album called *In Rainbows*? Y ☐ N ☐ DS ☐

6 Did *Radiohead* spend money on advertising? Y ☐ N ☐ DS ☐

RESPONDING TO THE TEXT

Do you agree or disagree with these sentences?

1 Buying music from the Internet is simple and quick.

2 Everybody should be able to share music online.

3 Jammie Thomas's fine was too large.

4 Large fines will stop others from sharing music illegally.

5 It's great to buy albums direct from a band's website.

6 Music companies will disappear.

SPEAKING

Talk to a partner and answer the questions.

1 Do you think CDs are too expensive? Do some people in the music business make too much money?

2 Are fines a good idea? Should parents pay fines for children who download music illegally?

3 Do you think it's OK for another student to copy your ideas or your homework? Would you feel angry or pleased?

PRONUNCIATION

Underline the stressed syllable in each of the adverbs. Then decide how many syllables the adverb has.

For example:

only _____2_____

1 nowadays _____   4 illegally _____

2 unfortunately _____   5 surprisingly _____

3 usually _____   6 clearly _____

WRITING

Write a short paragraph about digital downloads. Complete the text with your own comments.

I think downloading free music is ... because ... .

I think sharing music online is popular with young people because ... .

Another reason is ... .

EXERCISE 1

Read the text.

Doing Good

Claire's parents were not very happy when their daughter said she wanted to take time off. 'We thought it was more important that she went straight to university. However, she was very (1)_____ to go. The decision of what to do was (2)_____. She decided to work as a (3)_____ in a refugee camp. This is because she wanted to have a rewarding job and help others. She also wanted to (4)_____ her time away.'

What did they think when she came back? 'We were really pleased. She was much more (5)_____ and happy to work on her own. She said it was a (6)_____ job, but she was happy that it was difficult. She also made many friends. Now we think it was a good choice.'

EXERCISE 2

Choose a word or phrase to complete the paragraph. Use each word or phrase once only.

| up to her | challenging | make the most of |
| keen | independent | volunteer |

EXERCISE 3

Decide if the answers are Yes (Y), No (N), or if the test Doesn't Say (DS).

1 Was Claire away for a whole year?

Y ☐ N ☐ DS ☐

2 Did Claire's parents want her to go away?

Y ☐ N ☐ DS ☐

3 Did Claire choose what to do?

Y ☐ N ☐ DS ☐

4 Did she earn a lot of money?

Y ☐ N ☐ DS ☐

5 Was she a different person when she came back home?

Y ☐ N ☐ DS ☐

6 Does she want to work in a refugee camp again?

Y ☐ N ☐ DS ☐

EXERCISE 4

These words all have three syllables except one. Which word has four syllables?

1 important

2 decision

3 rewarding

4 refugee

5 independent

6 difficult

EXERCISE 1

Read the text.

The real thing

Not everyone is happy buying counterfeit goods. Sometimes, however, it's difficult to tell the difference between a fake Gucci bag and a real one. If you only want the real thing, follow these steps:

1 Don't go to a market. Genuine designer labels are not for sale in a market or on the street. The bags might look good, but they'll be copies.

2 Go to a good shop. Then, if you find out the bag is not real after all, they might give you your money back. A market stall holder will laugh at you!

3 Pay the full price. If it's cheap, it's a copy.

EXERCISE 2

Choose the correct word to make true sentences about the text.

1 Gucci bags for sale in a market are *probably / definitely* fake.

2 You buy a Gucci bag in a good shop and then realise it's a fake. The shop owner will *probably / definitely* give you your money back.

3 You buy a Gucci bag from the market and then realise it's a fake. The market stall holder will *probably / definitely* not give you your money back.

4 Cheap Gucci bags are *probably / definitely* fakes.

EXERCISE 3

Find the answers in the text. The answers are in this order in the text.

1 Which phrase means *some people are unhappy*?

2 Which adjective has a similar meaning to *fake*?

3 Which phrase means *to notice that something is not the same*?

4 Which phrase means *do these things*?

5 Which adjective has a meaning similar to *real*?

6 Gucci, Chanel, and Louis Vuitton are all examples of what?

7 Which noun has a meaning similar to a *fake*?

8 Who won't give you customer support?

EXERCISE 4

<u>Underline</u> the stressed syllable in each of these words.

1 everyone

2 counterfeit

3 difficult

4 difference

5 genuine

6 designer

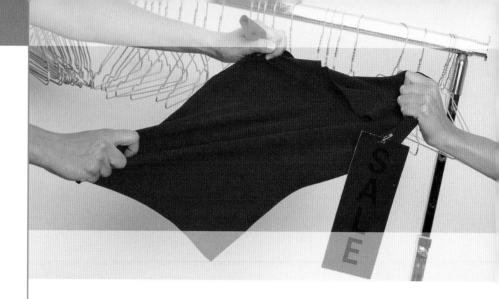

7 Accessories

The following verbs are all in the text. Put them into the past simple.

1 understand _____

2 begin _____

3 buy _____

4 go _____

5 spend _____

6 have _____

7 do _____

8 cut _____

Tick (✔) the things you spend your money on.

1 ☐ CDs / DVDs

2 ☐ going to the cinema / concerts

3 ☐ books and magazines

4 ☐ clothes

5 ☐ going to the hairdresser

6 ☐ make-up

7 ☐ going out with friends

8 ☐ something else – what?

Read about three students who tried not to spend their money on anything, except food and drink, for a month.

Doing without

George, 21: After just a few days I understood how difficult the task was. I also began to realise how powerful advertising is. After watching an ad for a new CD, for example, I want to go out and get it! To stop myself buying things I tried not to watch TV – there are just too many
5   ads. However, I bought some magazines and books – so that I could read instead of watching TV! I love going to the cinema, but I saved money by watching DVDs at home.

My friends often asked me out, and I couldn't say no for a whole month. Once we went ten-pin bowling and I spent a bit of cash that
10   evening. It's difficult to find activities to do that don't cost anything. I also had to buy a pre-paid card for my mobile, my alarm clock needed new batteries, and I had a haircut, too. The total I spent was £_____.

Sandra, 23: When I'm on my own it's not too bad, but it's difficult with friends because they always want to go shopping. The first two
15   weekends were hard; the last two weekends were impossible! I used my credit card to buy clothes – tops, a skirt, and two pairs of shoes. I also bought myself another pair of jeans. I know I don't need another pair, but they looked so nice. Then I paid for a jacket to go with the jeans, and bought some more sandals. I needed some shampoo, but I
20   bought loads of make-up at the same time.

My favourite band was also playing in concert, so I went to see them with my friends – I couldn't stop myself. Unfortunately, the price of the tickets was quite high because we wanted good seats, but it was worth it. I also went to the cinema a few times. Of course I didn't have to go
25   – but I love films!

Then it was my best friend's birthday, so of course I had to buy her a present. I also went to the hairdresser before the party. Now, at the end of the month, I see I have spent quite a lot of money. I'm a bit taken aback, especially as I was trying not to spend anything! My total was
30   £_____.

Benjamin, 19: There are just so many people trying to make you buy things! Advertising is the worst, of course – not just on TV, but also at bus stops, in magazines, in shops. It's difficult to ignore it. To help myself not buy anything unnecessary, I asked myself, 'Do I need this?
35   Do I really want this? Will my life be better if I buy this?' Of course the answer was always 'No'. I didn't have to buy anything, really. I could always do without it.

I like music, so it was hard not to buy any new CDs, but I decided
to listen to all the ones I don't play anymore – and in fact, there are
40 quite a lot. So listening to them made me feel I had something
new. I didn't waste money buying clothes, either – I realise I've got
enough at the moment. I watched my favourite DVDs, yet again,
instead of going to the cinema. My sister cut my hair and I could
borrow books and magazines from friends. My total for the month
45 was £_____.

COMPREHENSION 1 **How much do you think they spent? Match a figure with a name and write the amount in the text.**

1	George	**a**	£ 20
2	Sandra	**b**	£ 180
3	Benjamin	**c**	£ 900

Answer the questions with the name of one or two of the students.

4 Who realised that advertising makes you buy things?

5 Who went to the hairdresser?

6 Who had friends who were helpful?

7 Who tried to find ways of not buying things?

8 Who went to the movies?

COMPREHENSION 2 **Answer the questions.**

1 In line 2, another way of saying, *to begin to understand*
is _____.

2 In line 6, which phrase means *in place of something*?

3 In lines 15 to 17, which sentence is correct?

   a She bought some blouses, T-shirts, and other clothes on credit.

   b She bought some blouses, T-shirts, and other clothes with cash.

   c She bought some hats and other clothes on credit.

4 In line 18, why does Sandra buy the jacket?

   a She didn't have any jackets.

   b To match the jeans so that they look nice together.

   c To replace the jeans she bought.

5 In line 22, which phrase shows that Sandra had little control over buying the tickets?

6 In line 23, what does *but it was worth it* mean?

a Sandra was happy with the cost of the ticket because she had a good seat.

b Sandra thought the ticket was too expensive.

c Sandra thought the ticket was very cheap.

7 In lines 28 and 29, another way of saying *to be surprised* is
_____ .

8 In line 37, which phrase means *it wasn't necessary to have*?

9 In line 39, what does *ones* refer to?

a new CDs

b CDs he stopped listening to

10 In line 42, which phrase shows that Benjamin has seen his favourite DVDs many times?

COMPREHENSION 3 **Complete the sentences with the verbs from the text. Use each verb only once.**

| waste   spend   cost   get   save   pay |

1 It's my mum's birthday, so I'm going to _____ her a lovely present.

2 How did you _____ for this? By credit card or by cash?

3 I'm trying to _____ some money for a holiday this summer.

4 Don't _____ your money on buying things you don't need.

5 It's terrible, I _____ more money on travelling than going out.

6 How much did that _____? Was it expensive?

SPEAKING **Which views of the students are true for you? Tick (✔) the ones you agree with.**

George: ☐ *Advertising is very powerful.*

☐ *It's difficult to find activities that don't cost anything.*

Sandra: ☐ *My friends always want to go shopping.*

☐ *It's impossible not to buy any clothes.*

Benjamin: ☐ *It's difficult to ignore ads.*

☐ *I have a lot of CDs I don't listen to anymore.*

Grammar	*Could / couldn't*: for possibility in the past
Possibility/necessity in the past	*I bought books so I **could** read and not watch TV.* *I love films – I **couldn't** say no.*
	Had to / didn't have to: for necessity in the past *It was her birthday. I **had to** buy her something.* *I **didn't have to** go, but I really wanted to.*

GRAMMAR 1   Underline the best verb to complete the sentences.

1   I go to school by bus, so I (had to / didn't have to) buy bus tickets.

2   I (could / couldn't) stay in for a whole month, so I went out a few times.

3   I needed my mobile, so I (had to /didn't have to) buy a new pre-paid card.

4   The jeans were very expensive, but I (couldn't / didn't have to) stop myself.

5   My friends said I (could / had to) borrow their magazines if I wanted to.

6   I already have a lot of shoes, so I (couldn't / didn't have to) buy another pair, but I did!

GRAMMAR 2   Complete the paragraph using *could*, *couldn't*, *had to* or *didn't have to*.

We had no food in the house, so I (**1**)_____ go shopping. My father was very nice and said I (**2**)_____ use his car. That meant two things: I (**3**)_____ wait for the bus – and I (**4**)_____ buy more things! Unfortunately, the supermarket car park was full and I (**5**)_____ find a space. I (**6**)_____ wait ages for another car to leave.

Luckily there was a space near the entrance, so I (**7**)_____ walk too far.

SPEAKING   Talk to a partner and answer the questions.

1   Are you more like George, Sandra, or Benjamin? What kind of things do you buy that you don't really need?

2   Is it possible for you to buy nothing for a month? What things could you *not* do without?

3   What is your favorite ad?

Is it possible for you to buy nothing for a month?

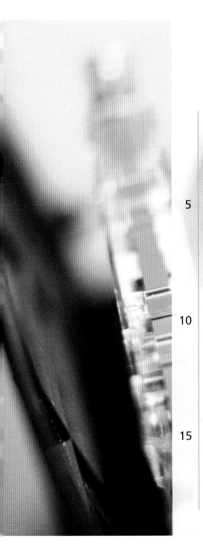

Effective • *Skills*

ACTIVATING
VOCABULARY

**Match a product to the words or phrases. Then check your
answers in the text.**

1 The personal stereo
2 The compact camera
3 The answerphone
4 The video recorder

a zoom lens
b recorded messages
c auto-reverse button
d cassette(s)
e 90 minutes
f slides and prints

First-generation gadgets

The personal stereo

My friends and I were very excited when we bought our Sony Walkmans in 1983. It was the first time we could listen to music wherever we were. The player was a little bigger than the cassette inside, and I usually clipped it onto my jeans. There was also an auto-reverse button, so that when the cassette
5 got to the end it automatically started to play the other side. That was just fantastic – I could listen to 90 minutes of music non-stop! I had a pair of earphones that went over my head and covered my ears.

The compact camera

I got my first compact camera in 1989. Like most cameras then it was a 35 mm, which was the size of the film it used. It was great – so easy to use:
10 everything was automatic including the focusing. It was an Olympus with a 70 mm zoom lens. I used different film – both slides and prints. When I put in the film for processing, I usually went back the next day to pick up the prints. I sometimes used black-and-white film because I like black-and-white images.

The answerphone

My mother hated it when I got my answerphone. She talked for ages before
15 she realised she was talking to a machine! I liked it because I knew who was calling me. If I didn't want to speak to that person, I didn't pick up the phone. Of course, people could also leave recorded messages (there was a tiny cassette inside), so I never missed anything important. I got mine in 1986, but I have no idea who made it.

> The video recorder
>
> 20 At the time it was a new and exciting idea: we didn't have to stay in when
> something good was on TV! We could go out, and then watch everything later or
> the next day. I remember we had a JVC, which I think we got in 1984, and it was
> very expensive at the time. However, it was worth it because we could decide on
> a better time to watch the programmes. By 1990, I had a huge collection of
> 25 recorded video-cassettes, and most of them were films.

SCANNING **Complete the table with information about the four products.**

Product	The name of the brand	The year it was bought
1 The personal stereo:		
2 The compact camera:		
3 The answerphone:	(n/g)	
4 The video recorder:		

READING FOR DETAIL **What did the person like *most* about the product?**

1 The personal stereo

    a You could listen to music anywhere.

    b You could wear it with jeans.

    c There was an auto-reverse button.

2 The compact camera

    a It was a 35 mm.

    b Everything was automatic.

    c You could use black-and-white film.

3 The answerphone

    a Your mother hated it.

    b It was possible to know who was calling.

    c People could leave messages.

4 The video recorder

    a You could choose when to watch programmes.

    b It was expensive.

    c You could record films on TV.

NOTICING VOCABULARY

<u>Underline</u> the word or phrase in each group that was *not* in the text. Then read again to check your answers.

1 The personal stereo

   very excited   listen to music   started to play   listen outside

2 The compact camera

   film   photographs   lens   prints

3 The answerphone

   talked for ages   pick up the phone   listen again
   never missed anything

4 The video recorder

   stay in   put on   go out   decide on

SPEAKING

Talk to a partner and answer the questions.

1 Can you still buy each of the four products today? Which one has changed the most?

2 Which product do you think is most useful to have? Why?

3 What are the main differences between these products from the 1980s, and the products you can buy today?

WRITING

Write about a product that you have. Say what brand it is, when you bought it, and why you like it.

I have a ... made by ... .

I bought it ... . I really like it because ... .

I also like it because ... .

8. Odd jobs

PRE-READING 1 **Put the following verbs in the correct order.**

to be accepted ☐

to have an interview ☐

to get paid ☐

to see a job advert 1

to start work ☐

to apply for a job ☐

PRE-READING 2 **Decide if the following are important to you in a job, or not important. Which is the most important?**

1 the number of hours you work a day

2 your promotion prospects

3 the people you work with

4 the money

5 the place where you work

6 the number of holidays

7 the chance to travel

8 how nice the boss is

Read about a student who did an unusual job one summer.

Extra work

Charlie: Students are used to finding jobs during the summer. The holidays are long, so there's plenty of time to get temporary work, and then go on a trip somewhere, before term starts. For a couple of summers I worked for the post office, and then, last summer, I became
5 a film star! Well, not actually a film star, but I was in a film.

It was August and I was visiting my parents, who live in a small town in the countryside. One day, I saw an advert for film extras in the local newspaper. A film company wanted to use the town as a location for their next film, and they wanted to employ lots of extras. You know,
10 those people in the background while the stars act in front of the cameras. For example, the other people in the restaurant eating, or the people running around screaming when there's a fire, or the people just walking down the road.

I thought it was a great idea. I wanted to meet some stars, and I also
15 wanted to see how a film was made. So I applied for the job and was really excited when I was accepted. There was no interview; they just said I looked all right. It was also quite a lot of money, which I'm not used to. The company wanted me to be an extra for one week of filming. They told me to arrive at 7.30 in the morning, so I got up very early and got there on time. There were lots of people on set, and I
20 spoke to some of the other extras. There were many different kinds of people – other students, business people, mothers and kids, and some tourists, too. We were all very excited. There was a lot of noise and action. The film crew was getting ready and preparing the set. This included setting up the lights, cameras, and recording equipment.

25 However, although the film crew were very busy, we were just waiting. Three hours later, we were still waiting. Now I'm used to doing nothing sometimes, but this was really boring. Finally, the director said he was ready to start shooting. Hurrah! He told us that a man was going to appear at a window. When we saw the man we had to shout 'No!' very
30 loudly and very often. After some more waiting, the camera operators finally started filming. The window opened, we saw the man, and we all shouted. Then we had to do it again and again. And again! I think we did that one scene 20 times!

35 This was a typical day. I arrived early each morning, and then waited and waited until the filming started. Then we always had to do the same scene again and again. After a few days, it became even more boring and I realised why I got paid quite a lot.

40 │ So what about the film stars? Well, I never saw them! The rest of the film was made in studios, or in other parts of the country. The scenes in my town didn't have any famous actors in them at all!

COMPREHENSION 1   **Here are three different summaries of the reading. Which one is correct?**

A Charlie worked as an extra in a film and thought it was fantastic. Every day was interesting and he met lots of film stars. The only bad thing was the money – he didn't get paid very much.

B Charlie worked as an extra in a film made in his town. All the local people were in the film. It was great fun and he got paid a lot of money, too.

C Charlie worked as an extra in a film. At first, he was very excited, but the work was quite boring, and he spent a lot of time waiting. The good thing was that he got paid quite well.

COMPREHENSION 2   **Answer the questions.**

1 In line 2, which phrase means, *a job for a short time*?

2 In line 9, another way of saying *to give someone a job* is _____?

3 In lines 11 to 14, what are *extras*?

    a The actors in a film
    b The people who are behind the actors
    c The camera operators

4 In line 14, what does *it* refer to?

    a being an extra
    b meeting stars
    c seeing how a film was made

5 In line 18, what time did Charlie arrive in the morning?

6 In line 25, what does *we* refer to?

    a the film crew
    b the actors
    c the extras

7 In lines 28 and 31, which two verbs have the same meaning?

8 In line 35, what is another way of saying *happening in the usual way*?

9 In line 38, why did Charlie get paid a lot?

    a because the work was very difficult

    b because the work was very boring

    c because film companies have lots of money

10 In lines 39 to 41, why didn't Charlie see the film stars?

    a There were no famous people in the film

    b They didn't come to his town

    c They were in different parts of the town

COMPREHENSION 3 **Match the words to make a phrase from the text.**

1	work	**a**	in front of the cameras
2	employ	**b**	ready to start shooting
3	scream	**c**	the recording equipment
4	act	**d**	when there's a fire
5	set up	**e**	for the post office
6	be	**f**	lots of extras

Read the text again and write the name of the subject for each of the above phrases.

1   *Charlie*

2   _____

3   _____

4   _____

5   _____

6   _____

Grammar	It's normal for students to get summer jobs.
Used to	*They are* **used to finding** *jobs.*
	It's strange for me to get paid a lot.
	I'm not **used to having** *a lot of money.*
	I'm not usually very busy.
	I'm **used to doing** *nothing.*
	Note: this structure only follows the verb *to be.*

GRAMMAR 1 **Complete the sentences with *used to* plus the verb in brackets to make true statements about the text.**

For example:

Students __*aren't used to having*__ (have) short summer holidays.

1 Charlie _____ (work) in the summer.

2 Film companies _____ (employ) extras.

3 Charlie _____ (work) in films.

4 Charlie _____ (wait) for three hours.

5 The camera operators _____ (film) the same scene many times.

6 Charlie _____ (meet) famous film stars.

GRAMMAR 2 **Use the prompts below and write some true sentences about yourself.**

1 live away / parents

2 talk / foreign students / English

3 get up early / weekends

4 meet / famous people

5 live / big city

6 work / holidays

SPEAKING **Talk to a partner and answer the questions.**

1 Charlie continued being in the film because he got paid a lot. What do you think is better: an interesting job with little money, or a boring job with lots of money? Why?

2 What kind of jobs would you like to do for a short time?

Effective •*Skills*

PRE-READING 1 **Match the names of the jobs with the descriptions.**

1   a checkout operator

2   a grape-picker

3   a bin man

4   a factory worker

5   a gardener

a   A person who works outside all year round. They grow plants and flowers.

b   A person who works in a supermarket. They take money from customers.

c   A person who works outside, usually in the summer. They pick fruit.

d   A person who works inside. They often use machines.

e   A person who collects rubbish.

Five students are talking about temporary work they did in the summer.

SUMMER JOBS

1 One summer holiday I worked in a factory. At the beginning I was really pleased, because the money was good. However, I had to do the same thing every day and it became very boring. I tried to think about interesting things, but this didn't help. The time went by so slowly. When I thought it was time for lunch, I realised it was only 10 o'clock! I had a contract for a month's work, but I left after a week.

5

2 I don't like being inside. When I'm sitting in lectures at university, I'm always staring out of the window and wanting to be outside. So I was really pleased when, one holiday, I got a job as a gardener in a large park. The work was quite hard and at the end of the day I was very tired, but that was fine. There were so many things to do with the plants, trees and grass. I was lucky, too, because the weather was warm and sunny.

10

3 I needed to pay for a holiday, so I decided to take a job in the local supermarket for a few weeks. I didn't really want to do the job, but there was no other work. I really didn't want to put things on shelves and stand up all day. However, I worked as a checkout operator, so that meant I could sit down! It was only for a few weeks, so it was fine, and I was really interested in what people bought!

15

20   **4** One September, I went to France to pick grapes. I wanted to work for a fortnight and then spend the money I earnt on a holiday. For the first few days it was very tiring work; the grapes were heavy and I walked a lot. Then, for the rest of the time, it rained every day, and I didn't get paid for not working. So at the end of the two weeks I
25   didn't have enough money to stay. That was a shame.

  5 My worst summer job was working as a bin man. First of all, I had to set off very early because we started work at 6 am. It was also very smelly work; some of the bins were disgusting, and I didn't want to touch them. The lorry smelt very bad, too. Moving the bins was also
30   quite difficult if they were very heavy. I always had a long, hot shower at the end of the day. The money was great, though, so I worked for a full month.

GENERAL UNDERSTANDING

Choose the correct ending (a-e) to make sentences about the text.

1	The factory worker	**a**	really liked the job
2	The gardener	**b**	really hated the job
3	The checkout operator	**c**	was disappointed
4	The grape-picker	**d**	left the job early
5	The bin man	**e**	was pleasantly surprised by the job

READING FOR DETAIL

Choose the correct sentence for each of the jobs.

1   **a**   The time went by slowly, so I had lunch at 10 o'clock.
     b   The job was really boring, so the time went very slowly.

2   **a**   Working in a park was hard work, but there were lots of interesting jobs to do.
     b   Working in a park was easy, but the weather was good.

3   **a**   I worked in a supermarket because there weren't any other jobs.
     b   I worked at the checkout because I wanted to stand up.

4   **a**   I picked grapes while I was on holiday in France.
     b   I didn't get any money while I wasn't working.

5   **a**   Although the job was really bad, I worked for four weeks.
     b   Although the bins were heavy and smelly, it wasn't a difficult job.

VOCABULARY IN CONTEXT **Find the words or phrases in the text that the students use.**

1 A noun that means *a written formal agreement* _____

2 A verb that means *to look at somebody or something for a long time* _____

3 An adjective that means *in the place where you live* _____

4 A noun that means *two weeks* _____

5 A verb that means *to begin a journey* _____

6 An adjective that means *very unpleasant, horrible* _____

SPEAKING **Talk to a partner and answer the questions.**

1 How do you usually spend the summer?

    a I do temporary work

    b I study

    c I have a holiday

    d Something else? What?

2 Which of the following temporary jobs would you not like to do? Can you explain why?

    hospital work

    post office work, for example, delivering letters

    farm work

    office work, for example, a secretary

    manual work, for example, a builder or fruit-picker

    factory work

    hotel work

    restaurant work

WRITING **Choose a temporary job for the summer and write a letter of application.**

I would like to work as a … during the summer.

I would like to do this job because …

Another reason is …

EXERCISE 1

Read the text.

Killer mobiles

When a London teenager found herself in a park during a bad electrical storm, she knew she had to stay away from the trees and not use her umbrella. She had her mobile phone with her so she could call her mum for help. Unfortunately, lightning hit the phone and she had a heart attack. Luckily, she survived but there have been cases of deaths during storms in Malaysia, Korea, and China. It seems that the metal parts in a mobile phone attract lightning. It's not even a good idea to have a mobile phone near you.

So next time it looks stormy, take a raincoat with you instead of a mobile phone.

EXERCISE 2

Decide if the sentences are True (T), False (F), or if the text Doesn't Say (DS).

1 It was necessary for the girl to be far from the trees.

T ☐ F ☐ DS ☐

2 It wasn't possible for her to telephone her mom.

T ☐ F ☐ DS ☐

3 The lightning killed the girl.

T ☐ F ☐ DS ☐

4 Storms in Asia are much worse than in Europe.

T ☐ F ☐ DS ☐

5 Phones that are made of plastic are safe to use in a storm.

T ☐ F ☐ DS ☐

6 It's a good idea to have both a raincoat and a mobile phone in a storm.

T ☐ F ☐ DS ☐

EXERCISE 3

Choose the correct verb to complete these sentences.

1 I'd love to get the latest iPod, but they just *spend / cost / pay* too much.

2 If you want to buy a new camera, then you should *get / save / pay* a little every month.

3 Most of my clothes are from the street market: you can *spend / waste / get* everything much cheaper there.

4 Don't *pay / waste / cost* your money on something that you'll never use.

5 The new job is much more interesting, but unfortunately they don't *pay / cost / save* me as much.

6 I *spend / pay / cost* most of my money on CDs and DVDs.

EXERCISE 1

Read the text.

Coffee break

Kate: One summer holiday I had a great **temporary** job. I worked as a 'barista' in a popular **local** coffee shop. Luckily, I didn't have to get up early in the morning. The shop opened at 7 am, but I started work at 10 am and usually finished at 7.30 pm. Ross, the owner, said he wanted to employ someone who likes coffee – and I love it! I can now make a perfect café latte, much better than the **disgusting** coffee my mum makes at home!

My **contract** was for only one month, but after a **fortnight**, Ross said I could work for two months. I didn't **earn** a lot, but it was such fun. Now I'm **used to** doing this I may open my own coffee shop when I leave university!

EXERCISE 2

Match a beginning and an ending to make true sentences about the text.

1 The coffee shop opened early	a so Ross said she could stay longer.
2 Kate said she loved coffee	b so she may do this as a full-time job.
3 Kate's mum makes coffee	c but she didn't earn a lot.
4 Kate worked well	d but Kate's coffee is better.
5 Kate enjoyed the job	e but Kate arrived later.
6 She is now experienced in the work	f so Ross gave her a job.

EXERCISE 3

Complete the sentences with a word in bold from the text.

1 I can smell bad eggs. It's _____.

2 My parents _____ a gardener once a week to cut the grass.

3 This is a _____ job; I'm only here for three months.

4 There are two meetings every month – once a _____.

5 Roger isn't _____ working outside all day, but he likes it now.

6 My _____ says I am allowed 20 days' holiday a year.

7 It's much easier for mum to walk to the _____ shops than to drive to the supermarket out of town.

8 Sandra and Pete both _____ £85,000 a year.

EXERCISE 4

Match the words in which the underlined o is pronounced the same

1	one	a	job
2	local	b	fortnight
3	coffee	c	month
4	morning	d	doing
5	who	e	owner

9 • Cybernauts

PRE-READING 1 **Put these phrases into the paragraph about different websites.**

social networking sites (n)

online games (n)

virtual world (n)

Internet (n)

addictive (adj)

When was the last time you went out and saw your friends? If it's a long time ago, perhaps you're spending too much time at the computer and on the (**1**) _____. There are many websites which are very (**2**) _____: it's impossible to leave them and do something else. Perhaps you like playing (**3**) _____, like *World of Warcraft*. Maybe you prefer (**4**) _____, where you can make hundreds of friends online. Or perhaps you like to live in a (**5**) _____, which can be more interesting than the real thing.

PRE-READING 2 **Name three ways people use the Internet to have fun.**

1 _____

2 _____

3 _____

Now read about people who love spending time on the Net.

Caught in the Net

1 Ahmed: Sometimes I think that *MySpace* has taken over my life. When I'm on the site I lose all sense of time. I have no idea how long I've been on it. I think it's just been a few minutes, but when I look at my watch it's been hours, not minutes! Sometimes I'm on the site

5 until the morning – and then I have to go to school and I feel terrible. I try to concentrate on my lessons, but all I really want to do is get back on *MySpace*! I now get very bad marks for my work, so I realise I've got a problem. *I just can't give it up!*

2 Lynne: I have problems getting on with my family; the virtual world

10 is so much easier. I don't have my mum getting at me about how untidy my room is, and I don't have to speak to my brother. I can do whatever I like! In *Second Life*, I'm another person: I have a new name and a new look. I wear fantastic clothes, I have beautiful hair, and I have lots of friends, too. _____

15 **3** Andrew: I spend every spare minute on *YouTube*, I'm afraid! I love music, and it's just the best way to watch concerts of my favourite bands and singers. There are some amazing videos of bands from the past, too, which are fun to watch. I also enjoy reading the comments that people make about the videos. *YouTube* is not just music, of

20 course. There are serious interviews, funny films of animals, dance, sport, and lots more. _____

4 Ana Belem: I love *Facebook* because it's the best way to stay in touch with friends and family. My parents love it, too. They don't complain that I don't email them very often these days: they can see my photos,

25 my videos and who my friends are. *Facebook* also tells me whose birthdays are coming up, so I always remember to send a card – an e-card, of course! The only problem is the amount of time I spend on *Facebook*. I sometimes spend more time on it than I do studying. _____

30 **5** Sae Ju: I became hooked on gaming when I was a student. I always played the heroic, handsome boy who fought monsters, and of course, had a beautiful girlfriend. I played endlessly, and I only stopped to eat or sleep. However, it soon affected my studies, and I stopped going to lectures. I said to myself, 'You won't get a degree and become

35 successful in the real world if you carry on playing games.' So I decided that I had to give it up. It was very difficult at first, but it was the right thing to do. _____

6 Rebecca: *Bebo* is great for so many reasons. It's very easy to understand – even my 12-year-old brother has no problems. I use it as

40 my very own web page, which I can change and add to as I want, and it's all free! *Bebo* is also great for contacting friends, and friends' friends – it's like one big party! Sometimes I think it's strange: I have a great social life, but I've never met my friends! _____

COMPREHENSION 1 **Complete the paragraphs with the missing last sentences.**

    A ~~I'm worried about my exam results now.~~

    B I just can't give it up!

    C Perhaps we should try getting together!

    D There's something for everyone!

    E So it's very different from my real life!

    F I realised these kinds of games can ruin your life.

COMPREHENSION 2 **Answer the questions.**

1 In line 2, what does the phrase *I lose all sense of time* mean?

    a I lose my watch so don't know what the time is.

    b I have absolutely no idea what the time is.

    c I do things very slowly.

2 In lines 5 to 6, another way of saying *I want to give all my attention to my lessons* is _____.

3 In lines 12 to 13, what does *I have a new look* mean?

    a I have a different appearance; I look different.

    b I now wear glasses, so I look different.

    c I see things in a new and different way.

4 In line 15, what phrase does Andrew use to show he's worried?

5 In line 20, which two adjectives have the opposite meaning?

6 In lines 23 and 25, what do Ana Belem's parents say?

    a Please email and let us know what you're doing!

    b Why don't you ever ring us?

    c We are happy that you are staying in touch.

7 In line 30, what does Sae Ju say about online gaming?

    a He found it boring to begin with.

    b He got addicted to it.

    c He didn't like it.

8 In line 33, what does *it* refer to?

    a the beautiful girlfriend

    b playing games all the time

    c stopping to eat or sleep

9 In lines 39, what does Rebecca say about her brother?

    a He has some problems using Bebo.

    b He likes using Bebo.

    c If he can use it, then it's very easy for her.

10 In line 43, what does Rebecca think is strange?

    a She has no friends.

    b She usually meets her friends online.

    c She only has virtual friends, not real ones.

COMPREHENSION 3   **Each of the sentences has a phrasal verb in bold. Which word or phrase has a similar meaning to the phrasal verb?**

1 All I want to do is **carry on** playing the game.

    a stop   **b** continue

2 I have problems **getting on with** my family.

    a liking and being friendly with   **b** speaking to

3 I don't like my mum **getting at** me.

    a saying nice things about me

    b always criticising or complaining about me

4 *Facebook* tells me when my friends' birthdays are **coming up**.

    a are about to happen soon

    b are about to arrive

5 I made myself **give up**.

    a stop   **b** stop having hope

6 I think *MySpace* has **taken over** my life.

    a destroyed   **b** taken control of

COMPREHENSION 4   **Complete the sentences with the phrasal verbs from the previous exercise.**

carry on   get on with   get at   take over   give up   come up

1 My sister is cooking lunch, so my mum is trying not to _____.

2 I'm afraid something urgent has _____, so I can't meet you today.

3 I hate my new school! I don't _____ with my classmates at all.

4 I know smoking is very bad for me, so I'm trying to _____.

5 I hope the teacher doesn't _____ me again for not doing my homework.

6 I don't want to do my homework; I want to _____ chatting online.

Give up

Get along with

Grammar	*stop doing* something – no longer do something
The infinitive (*to do*) or the gerund (*doing*)	I **stopped going** to lessons.
	stop to do something – stop so that something else can happen
	I only **stopped to eat** or sleep.
	try doing – see if this will help (a suggestion)
	We should **try getting together**.
	try to do – make an effort to do something
	I **try to concentrate** on my lectures, but I can't.

GRAMMAR 1   Underline the best verb to complete the sentences.

1   Mary stopped (to talk / talking) when the teacher came in.

2   If you have a headache, try (to drink / drinking) some water. That often helps.

3   Joe stopped (to take / taking) photos because his wife took enough for both of them.

4   There are some stunning views so try (to take / taking) a lot of good photos.

5   Sorry I'm late, but I stopped (to chat / chatting) with my sister.

6   I tried (to explain / explaining) the problem, but she talked non-stop.

GRAMMAR 2   Match the beginning of a sentence with an ending.

1   Sorry, I can't stop   a   reading, and listen to me.

2   I want to say something. Please stop   b   listening to this CD soon.

3   I promise I'll stop   c   to talk now, I'm really late.

Now do the same with these.

4   If you have a problem, try   d   to understand my views.

5   You never concentrate. Try   e   talking to a friend about it.

6   My parents never try   f   to listen more carefully.

SPEAKING   Which of these opinions from the text do you agree with? Explain why to another student.

1   Life in the virtual world is so much easier than real life.

2   Some websites are addictive, and spending too much time on the Net can be a serious problem.

3   These kinds of games can ruin your life.

4   People should stop meeting online and try meeting face to face.

Effective • *Skills*

Two other activities are also popular on the Internet. Decide which of the headings for each paragraph is correct.

1 Podcasting / Blogging / Programming

This is like having your own online diary or journal that everyone can read. You can write about anything (what you did today, why you like the colour orange, how to grow tomatoes), or you can write about anyone (your mum, the President of the USA, your lecturer).

2 Podcasting / Blogging / Programming

This is like having your own radio station that everyone can listen to. You can interview friends, chat about famous people, or report on what's happening in your neighbourhood. You can also use video, so then it's like having your own TV show that everyone can watch.

Read about Ben Curtis and match a question (A–E) with each of his replies.

A Who listens to the podcasts?

B Do you make money, or is it just a hobby?

C ~~Why did you decide to do podcasting?~~

D Is there anything else you'd like to add?

E Who do you talk to, and what do you talk about?

A **worldwide** audience

Ben Curtis, a podcaster with www.notesfromspain.com, says that the best thing about podcasting is that it's so simple. You only need a microphone, a computer, and something to share with the rest of the world. It's better than a radio programme: there are no transmitters, no satellites, and no regulations. Also, it's possible to reach more people in more areas of the world. Here he answers some questions about his website.

1 <u>*Why did you decide to do podcasting?*</u>

10 'I asked a friend what a podcast was because I had no idea. It sounded interesting so I thought I'd try to make one of my own. I became hooked immediately. I really loved being able to make radio programmes that I could then play to the world through the Internet.'

2 _____

'Most of the programmes involve me talking to my wife, Marina, 15 about life and culture in Spain. Now we have extended our podcasts to include a show about Spanish cooking, and another where we help people learn Spanish. It's hard work producing so many podcasts every month, but worth every minute of our time.'

3 _____

20 'People from all over the world! We've had emails from professors in Hawaii, people learning Spanish in New Zealand, and commuters in New York – it constantly amazes us to discover how far our podcasts travel!'

4 _____

25 'We make some money from the Spanish podcast by selling worksheets to help learners improve their language skills. So really it's a mixture of a hobby and a job at the moment. We hope to be making a living from it before too long.'

5 _____

30 'Podcasting and other technologies like blogging are changing the shape of world media. In the past it was just the big media companies that had a global voice, but now anyone can become a journalist and easily broadcast their thoughts all over the world. These are very exciting times!'

GENERAL UNDERSTANDING **Read the text again and <u>underline</u> the correct phrase for each sentence.**

1 Ben says that making a podcast needs *less equipment / more equipment* than making a radio programme.

2 At the beginning he *knew / didn't know anything* about podcasts.

3 The website was started for *learners of Spanish / people interested in Spain*.

4 Ben spends a *lot of time / not much time* producing the podcasts.

5 He wants to do podcasting *as a full time job / only as a hobby*.

6 He is *positive / negative* about how the media world is changing.

READING
FOR DETAIL

Decide if the sentences are True (T), False (F), or if the text Doesn't Say (DS).

1   Ben became addicted to podcasting very quickly.

2   Ben's wife is Spanish.

3   Ben's podcasts are listened to all over the world.

4   Listeners need to pay to learn about Spanish cooking.

5   Only big media companies have podcasts.

6   Ben has another job apart from podcasting.

SPEAKING

Talk to a partner and answer the questions.

1   Do you listen to any podcasts or read any blogs? Say which ones and explain why.

2   Imagine you have a podcasting website

  a   what subject would you talk about and

  b   who would you interview?

PRONUNCIATION

Underline the word in each group that has a different *O* sound?

1   n<u>o</u>tes   fr<u>o</u>m   d<u>o</u>t   c<u>o</u>m

2   microph<u>o</u>ne   <u>o</u>ne   radi<u>o</u>   gl<u>o</u>bal

3   p<u>o</u>dcasting   bl<u>o</u>gging   j<u>o</u>b   w<u>o</u>rk

4   m<u>o</u>ment   s<u>o</u>mething   l<u>o</u>ved   m<u>o</u>ney

5   wh<u>o</u>   d<u>o</u>   n<u>o</u>   t<u>o</u>

WRITING

Design your own podcasting website. Describe the site to a friend in an email.

| To: | | cc: | | Subject: | |

I have my own podcast site! The name of the site is

_____. I mainly talk about _____ but

I also talk about _____. I interview people,

for example _____ and _____. I think

podcasting is great because _____.

10 · Skincare

Name a job (or jobs) that uses the following.

1 a needle   _____

2 a drill   _____

3 plastic gloves   _____

4 a lorry   _____

5 camouflage   _____

6 jewellery   _____

Put these situations in order of how nervous they make you feel from 1 to 8, with 1 as the most nervous.

1 taking an exam   ☐

2 waiting to see the dentist   ☐

3 watching a horror film   ☐

4 being at home all alone   ☐

5 having a disagreement with your parents   ☐

6 waiting to see the doctor   ☐

7 speaking to people you don't know   ☐

8 something else – what?   ☐

Marked for life

Julia's in a waiting room, and she's looking nervous. She can see a man sitting very still with his sleeve rolled up and a woman nearby wearing plastic gloves and a white coat. She's also holding a needle. Is Julia waiting to see the doctor? No, she's not. Now there's the
5 sound like a small drill; perhaps she's waiting to see the dentist? Not that either. In fact, the woman in the white coat is a tattooist, and Julia's waiting to have her first tattoo.

'I don't know why I'm so nervous!' Julia laughs. 'I'm only going to have a small tattoo. It's going to be here, on my shoulder, so I know
10 that it won't hurt – well, not too much anyway! It only really hurts if the tattoo is done on skin over bone, like on your foot.'

'Some people think I might not like my tattoo in the future, but I disagree. I know that the people who regret having a tattoo are those who chose the name of their boyfriend, for example, and
15 then they split up. I'm going to have a picture of a small dolphin, because I love the sea – and I'm sure I'll always love the sea! I dislike this fashion of having an Asian tattoo, especially if the Chinese or Japanese characters mean something different from what you think they do. I have a friend who thought she had the
20 Chinese character for "beauty" on her back, but in fact it said "ugly". She was really dismayed when she found out.'

Julia says that most of her friends now have a tattoo. 'I think they're popular for a number if reasons. One is because it's much easier to have them done safely these days. It's much cheaper to have them
25 done on holiday here in Asia, too; it's much more expensive back in the UK. Also, the association with criminals and lorry drivers is disappearing. Plus, of course, it's now quite trendy, especially as stars like Angelina Jolie have tattoos.'

'However, there's still something "naughty" or "bad" about having a
30 tattoo. It's something that parents might disapprove of. This makes it appealing for young people like me; it's a form of rebellion. I'm not really sure what my parents will say when they see it; I just hope they won't be too disappointed.'

Julia's also interested in the history of tattooing. 'I like the idea that
35 it's an art form that's been around for thousands of years and done all over the world. However, the reasons for the tattoos and the designs vary a lot. In Indonesia, members of the Iban tribe were covered in tattoos of plants and animals for camouflage as they went hunting in the jungle; the Maori in New Zealand tattooed their faces

40 | to make themselves look aggressive when fighting; it's an ancient
Hindu-Buddhist custom still practised today; and it's associated with
organised gang crime in Japan.'

Why does Julia want a tattoo? 'I hope I'll look more attractive! I see it
as a kind of decoration, like jewellery – the difference being I can
45 | never take it off!'

COMPREHENSION 1   **Decide if the answers are Yes (Y), No (N), or if the text Doesn't Say (DS).**

1 Is Julia waiting to see the dentist?   Y ☐ N ☐ DS ☐

2 Does she want a tattoo on her foot?   Y ☐ N ☐ DS ☐

3 Does she have a boyfriend?   Y ☐ N ☐ DS ☐

4 Is it cheaper to have a tattoo done in Asia than
   in the UK?   Y ☐ N ☐ DS ☐

5 Do her parents know she's having a tattoo done?   Y ☐ N ☐ DS ☐

6 Are tattoos a modern invention?   Y ☐ N ☐ DS ☐

COMPREHENSION 2   **Read the text again. Then match a *noun or phrase* in column A with a *description* in column B to a *reason* in column C.**

A	B	C
1 Julia	1 a small dolphin	1 for camouflage
2 a man	2 trendy	2 she's waiting to have a tattoo
3 Julia's tattoo	3 very still	3 to look aggressive
4 the Iban tribe	4 tattooed faces	4 film stars have them
5 having a tattoo	5 nervous	5 she loves the sea
6 the Maori	6 tattooed all over	6 he's having a tattoo

COMPREHENSION 3   **Answer the questions.**

1 In lines 10 and 11, what does Julia say about having a tattoo on the foot?
   a It can cause physical pain.
   b It can make you laugh.
   c It doesn't cause any physical pain.

2 In lines 13 to 15, which people feel sorry about having a tattoo?
   a people with tattoos of their boyfriend's name who then get married
   b people with tattoos of their boyfriend's name who then end the
      relationship
   c people who don't have tattoos of their boyfriend's name

3 In line 18, what popular tattoo design does Julia mention?

   a the name of a person in a book, play, or film

   b a description of someone's personality

   c an Asian letter, number, or symbol

4 In lines 26 and 27, what connection is disappearing?

   a the one between criminals and lorry drivers and having a tattoo

   b the one between film stars and having a tattoo

   c the one between criminals and film stars

5 In lines 22 to 28, how many reasons does Julia give for tattoos being popular?

6 In line 29, which two words have a similar meaning?

7 In line 31, which phrase describes tattooing as a way of going against what parents want or accept?

8 In lines 35 and 36, why is Julia interested in the history of tattooing?

   a She likes modern art.

   b It's a global practice with an interesting past.

   c She likes travelling to different parts of the world.

9 In lines 40 and 41, which sentence is correct?

   a Tattooing is a very old Hindu-Buddhist tradition.

   b Tattooing is no longer done in Asia.

   c Tattooing is a bad Hindu-Buddhist habit.

COMPREHENSION 4 **Complete the sentences from the text with words that begin with *dis-*, for example, '*disagreement*'.**

In which words is *dis-* not a prefix?

1 Some people think I might not like my tattoo in the future.
I _____.

2 I _____ this fashion of having an Asian tattoo. I think it looks awful.

3 She was really _____ when she found out her tattoo meant *ugly* in Chinese.

4 The association with criminals and lorry drivers is _____.

5 A tattoo is something that parents might _____ of.

6 I just hope my parents won't be too _____.

Grammar	*going to* – a plan for the future, reporting a decision
Future plans and predictions	I'**m going** to have a small tattoo.
	It'**s going** to be a picture of a small dolphin.
	will – a *prediction* of what might happen in the future
	I'm sure I'**ll** always love the sea.
	I hope they **won't** be too disappointed.

GRAMMAR 1   **Complete the sentences about future plans or predictions with *is* or *are going to* or *will* or *won't*.**

1   Julia's friend wants a tattoo; she _____ have a picture of a star.

2   Julia hopes that the tattoo _____ hurt too much.

3   Angelina Jolie already has a lot of tattoos, but perhaps she _____ have some more.

4   Maybe Julia's parents _____ think the tattoo looks nice.

5   After having her tattoo done, Julia _____ write emails to her friends at home because she wants to tell them all about it.

6   She _____ send some photos of the tattoo as well.

GRAMMAR 2   **What are your plans and ideas for the future? Complete the table with what you are going to do, and what you hope or think you'll do.**

Plans and decisions (going to)	Predictions (will)
When I finish college I'm going to work for my father.	I hope it'll be interesting.

SPEAKING   **Complete the following sentences with your opinion. Then explain your opinion to another student.**

I think having a tattoo is …

1   I think having a tattoo is …

    a sexy   **d** dangerous

    b a stupid thing to do   **e** something else – what?

    c trendy

2   If I have a / another tattoo it's going to be …

    or I know I'll never have a tattoo because …

Effective • *Skills*

ACTIVATING
THE TOPIC **Answer the questions below and compare your answers with another student.**

1 In general, who do you think takes longer to get ready in the morning: men or women?

2 How long does it take you to get ready?

3 Do you like people looking at you?

4 What is a metrosexual? A city man who is in love with…

   a women   **b** men   **c** his appearance   **d** life

SKIMMING AND
SCANNING **Read the text quickly and match a question (A–F) with the answers in the text.**

A How many shirts do you have?

B Do you buy any hair products?

C How much do you spend a month on looking good?

D How often do you go to a spa?

E ~~How long does it take you to get ready for work or class in the morning?~~

F Do you buy any skin products?

Are You Metrosexual?

Is it true that many men are metrosexual? Three men agreed to do a questionnaire for *Today's Man* magazine; here are their answers.

1 *How long does it take you to get ready for work or class in the morning?*

   A: It can take up to 40 minutes. Hairstyling takes quite a long time, as well as choosing what to wear.

   B: 10 minutes at the most! I have a quick shower and throw on some clothes, then I'm out the door!

   C: Probably 20 minutes to shower, shave, and get dressed.

2 _____?

   A: More than £400. That includes new designer clothes, gym membership, and trips to the hairdresser.

   B: About £30. My mum usually buys my clothes, but I'll buy myself a new pair of jeans or a shirt every so often.

   C: It depends, on average £60, perhaps more. I like to look quite sharp and for a special occasion I'll spend more.

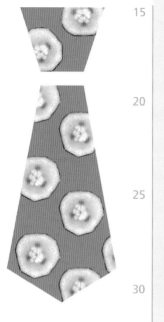

15

3 _____ ?

A: At least 40 – all different colours and styles. Most are designer labels.
B: Seven, I think. I prefer wearing T-shirts.
C: Fifteen? I'm not sure.

4 _____ ?

20

A: Certainly. I buy eye creams, facial masks, and moisturisers. I have one moisturiser for the day and another one for the night.
B: Never! That's for women only!
C: I buy aftershave and hand and body lotion.

5 _____ ?

25

A: Although I regularly go to the hairdresser, I still have a lot of creams, lotions, brushes, and a hair drier.
B: Of course – I buy shampoo!
C: I buy shampoo, conditioner, and gel.

6 _____ ?

30

A: A lot! I love massages and regularly go to an all-male spa. I feel fantastic afterwards.
B: No way! My friends would laugh at me if they found out.
C: Never. I keep thinking I might give it a try, but not yet.

READING FOR DETAIL **Read about the three men who answered the questions.**

Matt, 25, accountant

When I go out in the evening with my girlfriend, she always looks nice so I try to look good, too. I'm often much more casual at the weekend, though.

Carlos, 21, student

I don't have too much money to spend on clothes, but I don't think that's a problem. Men shouldn't look like fashion models when they go out.

Luigi, 29, magazine photographer

I think women today want men with good skin and good bodies. I spend more money on my clothes and cosmetics than my girlfriend does!

Match the name of a man with the answers A, B, or C in the text. Which man is metrosexual?

1 Matt gave all the ___ answers.

2 Carlos gave all the ___ answers.

3 Luigi gave all the ___ answers.

VOCABULARY
IN CONTEXT

Match a noun in column A with a noun in column B to make compound nouns from the text.

A	B
1 designer	a lotion
2 gym	b drier
3 eye	c clothes
4 body	d cream
5 hair	e model
6 fashion	f membership

SPEAKING

Talk to a partner and answer the questions.

1 Which man gave the best replies: Matt, Carlos, or Luigi? Why do you think so?

2 Which of these two opinions do you agree with the most? Why?

 a Men shouldn't look like fashion models when they go out.

 b I think women today want men with good skin and good bodies.

3 Do you agree that many men nowadays are metrosexual? Why / why not?

WRITING

Write to the magazine with your opinion. Do you think that it's OK for men to spend a lot of time and money looking good? Or is this only for women? Which of the three men do you agree with?

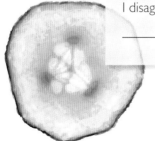

I think that looking good is very / not important for men. I agree with

_____ because I think _____.

I disagree with _____ because I think _____

_____.

EXERCISE 1

Read the text about Graham, who has his own blog about Vietnamese food.

The blogger

Graham answers questions about his blog: noodlepie.com

1 _____
'I discovered FatMan Seoul, a blog about food in Seoul, and realizsd that was exactly what I wanted to do in Saigon.'

2 _____
'That was easy as, living in Vietnam, especially Saigon, you're surrounded by good food. I love food, so it was the most natural topic for me.'

3 _____
'A lot of very different people, from other food bloggers to editors, famous food writers, chefs, and lots of Vietnamese living abroad who miss Vietnamese food.'

4 _____
'Yes, a lot through advertising on the site. Also I get asked at least once a month to write an article for a magazine about food.'

5 _____
'Blogging can get very addictive!'

EXERCISE 2

Match a question with each of Graham's replies. One question is not needed.

A Who reads your blogs?

B Do you make any money?

C Why did you decide to have a blog?

D Where do you live?

E Is there anything else you'd like to add?

F Why did you choose that subject?

EXERCISE 3

Complete the sentences with the words or phrases in the box.

| journal online games role-playing |
| virtual addicted to witchcraft |

1 'I'll be the king, and you can be the princess.'
   'Oh no, I hate _____!'

2 Graham says it's possible to get _____ blogging.

3 Blogging is like having your own _____ that everyone can read.

4 My favourite games have a lot of bad magic. You know – _____.

5 I know some people who sit at the computer for hours and hours playing _____.

6 Lynne thinks the _____ world is better than real life.

EXERCISE 1 Off-white

Read the text.

Ms T disliked her brown skin; she wanted to look like a film star, and Asian film stars have white skin. She decided to try a special face cream that promised a beautiful white face. However, she was dismayed when she looked in the mirror. Instead of the brown disappearing, her skin had become pink and dark brown. Ms T and her boyfriend then split up following a disagreement about the skin product. She began to regret using the cream, especially when she lost her job as a waitress in a restaurant.

'I'm really disappointed with the results. I have no job, no boyfriend, and an ugly face,' says Ms T.

EXERCISE 2

Find the answers in the text. The answers are in this order in the text.

1 Which verb means *not like*?

2 Which adjective means *sad about something that is surprising or shocking*?

3 Which verb means *to become impossible to see*?

4 Which verb means *to end a romantic relationship*?

5 Which noun means *a situation in which people have different opinions*?

6 Which verb means *to feel sorry about something you have done*?

7 Which adjective means *unhappy because something did not happen as expected*?

8 Which adjective is the opposite of *beautiful*?

EXERCISE 3

Complete the sentences using *but, because,* or *so* to make true sentences about the text.

1 Ms T didn't like the colour of her skin _____ she tried to change it.

2 She wanted white skin _____ Asian film stars have white skins.

3 She tried a special face cream _____ the results were bad.

4 Her skin changed colour _____ it didn't become white.

5 She lost her job _____ she didn't look very nice anymore.

6 Ms T's life is worse than before, _____ she is really unhappy.

EXERCISE 4

Decide if the first or second syllable of these words is stressed.

1 promised ● • / • ●

2 regret ● • / • ●

3 decide ● • / • ●

4 result ● • / • ●

5 ugly ● • / • ●

11 · Sports: past and present

PRE-READING 1 Complete the sentences about football with the verbs in the past tense. Use each verb only once.

beat   draw   win   send off   lose   be

1 Spain _____ to France in the quarter-finals.

2 Italy _____ the World Cup in Germany.

3 Portugal and Croatia _____ 0-0 in the opening match.

4 At half-time Qatar _____ in the lead.

5 Chelsea _____ Manchester United 4-1 yesterday.

6 The referee _____ two players in last night's match.

PRE-READING 2 <u>Underline</u> the word that does not belong in each group.

1 goalkeeper	striker	fan	substitute	football player
2 field	ticket	ball	net	half-way line
3 half-time	full-time	injury time	extra time	overtime
4 score	shoot	kick	result	head
5 crowd	red card	whistle	referee	penalty
6 qualifying round	knockout stage	trophy	semi-finals	final

Goal!!!

1 _____

July 1966

The North Korean football team shocked the world yesterday by beating the mighty Italians 1-0. It was an amazing match and the Korean team has gone from strength to strength, first losing against the USSR, then equalising against Chile, and now beating the Italians. Pak Do Ik's goal means two things. The favourites are out of the World Cup, and North Korea now faces Portugal in the first knockout stage.

2 _____

June 1969

Only hours after El Salvador's 3-2 win over Honduras, fighting broke out across the border between the two countries. Both teams were in Mexico yesterday for their third match to find out who qualifies for next year's World Cup finals. As both teams have won a game, this was the decider. There have already been disagreements between the two countries with acts of violence. Last night was the first time a battle on the football field turned into political combat.

3 _____

June 1986

A controversial win for Argentina has knocked England out of this year's World Cup. During the quarter-final in Mexico City, Maradona clearly used his hand to put the ball past the goalkeeper and into the net. The Tunisian referee allowed the goal despite English protests. After the match Maradona referred to the hand of God. He went on to score an incredible goal, having collected the ball from the halfway line and passing most of the English team. Argentina won 2-1 and now go through to the semi-finals against Belgium.

4 _____

July 1994

100,000 Colombians were at the funeral of Andrés Escobar, the murdered football player, yesterday afternoon. Escobar was leaving a restaurant with his girlfriend when he was shot in the chest and face. Three men went for the football player, shouting about his own goal.

It was during the World Cup match against the United States that Escobar scored an own goal. The Americans won 2-1 and the Colombians didn't qualify for the next round. Nine days later Escobar was dead.

5 _____

May 2005

A crowd of 65,000 in Istanbul saw Liverpool win the Champions League after being three goals down at half time. AC Milan scored in the first minute, and after 45 minutes, the Italians in the crowd already thought the cup was theirs. However, in an amazing turnaround, Liverpool equalised after just 59 minutes. In a penalty shootout the Reds went on to win 3-2 to claim the trophy for the fifth time.

35

6 _____

July 2007

40

Saudi Arabian fans looked on in horror as their team lost 1-0 in the Asian Cup final in Jakarta. The favourites were beaten by Iraq, who turned out to be the better team in their first visit to the finals. Younis Mahmoud headed the winning goal in the last ten minutes of the match and gave his country something to celebrate. It's the first time Iraq has won a tournament; they can now enjoy being the champions until the next Asian Cup in Qatar in 2011.

45

COMPREHENSION 1   **Match a heading with each of the newspaper articles.**

A World Cup Tragedy   **D** A Football War

B Hand of God   **E** An Asian Surprise

C An All-Arab Final   **F** Italians See Red

COMPREHENSION 2   **Answer the questions.**

1 In line 3, another way of saying, _to get stronger_ is _____.

2 In line 5, who are _the favourites_?

   a The Koreans   **b** The Italians   **c** The Russians

3 In line 14, which two words mean the same as _a fight_?

4 In lines 15 to 19, how did people feel about Argentina winning?

   a There were strong feelings of happiness.

   b Everyone thought it was a fair game.

   c There were strong feelings of disagreement.

5 In line 18, what did the referee do?

   a He ignored English protests and said the goal was OK.

   b He listened to English protests and said the goal was not OK.

   c He gave Argentina a penalty shot.

6 In line 27, who was shouting?

   a the attackers   **b** Escobar

7 In line 29, what does *It* refer to?

    a the shooting   **b** the own goal   **c** the funeral

8 In lines 36 and 37, which phrase shows that there was a very surprising change in the match?

9 In line 40, what does *looked on in horror* mean?

    a watched the match and were terrified

    b watched the match and were surprised and happy

    c watched the match and were surprised and shocked

COMPREHENSION 3 **Each of the sentences has a phrasal verb in bold. Which word or phrase has a similar meaning to the phrasal verb?**

1 Fighting **broke out** among the fans.

    a escaped   **b** started

2 The gunmen **went for** Escobar outside a restaurant.

    a attacked   **b** chose

3 The Iraqis **turned out** to be the better team.

    a finished   **b** proved

4 It was the match to **find out** who qualified.

    a get information about   **b** look for

5 After coming out on top of the group, England **went through** to the second round.

    a advanced to another stage   **b** examined carefully

6 Maradona **went on to** score an incredible goal.

    a continued without stopping

    b did something after completing something else

COMPREHENSION 4 **Complete the sentences with the phrasal verbs from the previous exercise.**

> broke out   went for   turned out   find out
> went through   went on to

1 Let's _____ who won the match last night.

2 The hooligan _____ the Italian supporter with a knife.

3 They equalised against Chile and then _____beat Italy.

4 Last night a fire _____ in the stadium.

5 He _____ to be one of the world's best players.

6 Arsenal _____ to the Champions League but lost to Barcelona in the final.

> **Grammar**
>
> Past simple and present perfect
>
> *Past simple – past, finished <u>and</u> we know when*
> North Korea **shocked** the world **yesterday**.
> **Last night** we **saw** a battle on the field.
> France **didn't play** their best **in the game**.
>
> *Present Perfect – if an event is not past or finished*
> Spain **have played** well during this competition.
>
> *Present perfect – we don't know when*
> Both teams **have won** a game.

GRAMMAR 1 **Decide if the verbs in the sentences are past simple or present prefect.**

1 On 15 June, El Salvador _____ (beat) Honduras 3-0.

2 Now both countries _____ (lose) one game each.

3 Klose _____ (score) 5 goals in the 2006 World Cup.

4 Who _____ (score) more goals: Ronaldo or Pélé?

5 Barcelona _____ (win) the Champions League in 2006.

6 Other Spanish teams _____ (win) the League as well.

GRAMMAR 2 **Complete the paragraph with the verbs in the box in the past simple or present perfect.**

> to be (twice)   to play (twice)   to win   to draw

Who will win – Portugal or Italy? Well, I think Portugal
(**1**)_____ fantastic all through this competition.
Italy (**2**)_____ really well in the game against Turkey,
but (**3**)_____ weak when playing against Tunisia. I know
that Italy (**4**)_____ all their matches in the first round
and that Portugal (**5**)_____ 0-0 against Ghana. However,
I still think that in general Portugal (**6**)_____ better so far
during this competition. So I think the Portuguese will win.

SPEAKING **Talk to a partner and answer the questions.**

Which statement do you agree with and why?

a Football is great! The World Cup helps us to understand each other better.

b I hate football! The players always cheat.

c I'm not interested in football at all. The World Cup is boring.

d None of the above. I think football is _____.

Effective • *Skills*

PREDICTING Linda rode a Zorb® globe in New Zealand, and Jeff tried kitesurfing in Indonesia. Which of the comments below do you think are Linda's, and which are Jeff's? Look at the pictures to help you.

1 I ache all over!

2 I only did a few jumps.

3 I was in the middle!

4 Suddenly, I was going round and round…

5 I fell over a lot.

6 It's really weird.

HAVE A GO!

Linda: This is a great holiday – last week I did something really mad: I rode a Zorb® globe! A Zorb® globe is a huge inflatable ball. It's about 3 m in diameter and there are two layers of plastic, 70 cm apart. This area between the two layers is filled with air, so it looks like a big balloon with a
5 hole in the middle – and that's where I was, in the middle! Inside there's a harness that you strap yourself into. That's because the ball rolls down a hill! Suddenly I was going round and round, up and down, over and over – wow! I was safe because of the air between the layers, but a Zorb® globe can go as fast as 50 kilometres an hour! However, the ball's so big it
10 doesn't feel very fast. It's really weird – 10 seconds of floating on air!

It's cheaper to go down with someone else, but I paid NZ$45 (about £14) and the same amount to do it again!! You can't buy a Zorb® globe, so I won't bring one back home with me!

Jeff: I can't walk! No – I'm not ill, I went kitesurfing
15 yesterday, and I ache all over – but I had a great time! It's like windsurfing and kite flying together. My 3-hour beginner's lesson cost £50. I had a board about 1.5 m long and a huge inflatable kite that was about 12 m wide. I was also strapped
20 into a harness. This is because you can jump into the air – although I never did any big

25 jumps. It's also possible to go over 40 knots (over 70 km/h) but again I didn't go that fast – you have to be really strong to control the kite. I fell over a lot, but luckily, the sea was warm! Also, more experienced kitesurfers can surf for a couple of hours, but after 30 minutes I was exhausted!

It's not a cheap sport – If you want to have all your own stuff then it costs at least £1,000, but of course, you can buy everything secondhand. But I think I'm sticking to beach volleyball when I get back!

SCANNING   Complete the table with information about the two sports.

	Riding a Zorb	Kitesurfing
1 When did they do the sport?		
2 What size is the equipment?		
3 How fast is it possible to go?		
4 How long do the sports take?		
5 How much did they pay?		
6 Is it a land or water sport?		

VOCABULARY IN CONTEXT 1   **Answer the questions. The words in bold are from the text.**

1   Which object isn't **inflatable**: a life jacket, a football, a golf ball, or a tyre?

2   Which sport doesn't need a **harness**: rock climbing, skiing, parachuting, or bungee jumping?

3   Which object doesn't have **straps**: a computer, a helmet, a seat belt, or a rucksack?

4   Which object can't be bought **secondhand**: a radio, a sandwich, a camera, or a coat?

5   Which sport can you do alone without being **experienced**: scuba diving, rock climbing, sailing or running?

Which object isn't inflatable?

VOCABULARY IN CONTEXT 2 | **The text has different adjectives to describe size. Choose the best adjective to complete the sentences: *big*, *great* or *huge*.**

1 There was a _____ crowd – perhaps more than a million people.

2 Rooney had problems because he hurt his _____ toe.

3 Luckily, he's in _____ form now and playing very well.

4 However, it was a _____ pity that Owen couldn't play.

5 Some professional football players earn _____ money.

6 I hope Pélé lives to a _____ age.

SPEAKING | **Talk to a partner and answer the questions.**

1 Which sport would you like to try: riding a Zorb or kitesurfing? Why?

2 Which sports do you prefer: more traditional sports (eg football, tennis, etc) or new sports (eg bungee jumping, riding a Zorb, etc). Why?

3 Is there a sport that you usually do? If yes, what is it?

PRONUNCIATION | **Underline the word that has a different sound in each group.**

1 b<u>a</u>ll   b<u>a</u>lloon   w<u>a</u>lk   <u>a</u>lso

2 h<u>o</u>le   r<u>o</u>lls   contr<u>o</u>l   v<u>o</u>lleyball

3 f<u>i</u>lled   h<u>i</u>ll   k<u>i</u>lometre   w<u>i</u>ld

WRITING | **Choose a new sport you want to try. It can be a Zorb, kitesurfing or something else. Explain why you want to have a go.**

I want to try … .

This is because I think … is … .

Also I think … .

12 · From cover to cover

PRE-READING 1 **Put a tick (✔) by the things you prefer to read and give an example.**

academic papers	☐	_____
advertisements	☐	_____
brochures	☐	_____
catalogues	☐	_____
comics	☐	_____
letters / emails	☐	_____
magazines	☐	_____
manuals	☐	_____
newspapers	☐	_____
paperbacks	☐	_____
reference books	☐	_____
websites	☐	_____
graded readers	☐	_____
Something else - what?	☐	_____

PRE-READING 2 **Decide what kind of reading material you think these people may be interested in. Then read about them.**

1   man, aged 42, IT technician

2   woman, aged 35, housewife

3   man, aged 27, journalist

4   woman, aged 22, student

5   man, aged 19, student

6   girl, aged 14, student

What's that you're reading?

1 I'm mad about gardening; it helps me to relax and forget about the office. I don't have a garden, but I grow plants, and vegetables, too, on our balcony. Every month I get a gardening magazine which I subscribe to. It's full of practical hints, topical news, and interesting features. There are articles by famous gardeners who also reply to readers' questions. I spend a lot of time looking up how to grow things on different websites, too, and many seed catalogues are online now.

2 I took up golf a few years ago and now play at least twice a week. I have a monthly subscription for a golf magazine that I love reading. There's advice on golf fashion and articles about golfing stars, as well as instruction on how to be a better player. There are also features on golf courses around the world and tons of advertisements and reviews on the latest equipment. I'm either playing golf or reading about it!

3 Of course, I have to keep up-to-date with all the news and views around the world, so I spend a lot of time browsing websites for the latest information. I also skim the main articles in newspapers. I'm also teaching myself French and have a course book and a dictionary for that. I read French graded readers too – these are novels written in simplified French: there's a glossary at the back and exercises. They're really helping me to improve!

4 I have a lot of exams coming up, so I spend a lot of time studying for those. I have to read up on a number of different subjects and spend quite a lot of time in the library. When I'm bored, I look at various fashion magazines, although I don't usually read the articles. I just like the pictures. If my friends are around, I'll read out the horoscopes to see if any of us are going to meet Mr Right!

5 I'm addicted to *manga*! It's terrible; I spend a small fortune buying loads of *manga* magazines – I just can't stop myself! I love drawing my favourite characters, too; my notebooks are full of sketches instead of things my lecturers have said! I try to read the books for my course, but I find myself skipping pages, and it's difficult to concentrate. I don't like reading things without any pictures.

6 Most of what I read, apart from schoolbooks, of course, are the emails and text messages from my friends. We send lots of messages to each other. My mum never understands what my friends are saying! I also go to a couple of chat rooms on the Internet. The only other thing I look at is the *TV Guide* – I scan it to see if my favourite programmes are there. If not, I'm back on the computer again. Perhaps that's why my spelling is so bad!

(Line numbers in margin: 5, 10, 15, 20, 25, 30, 35)

COMPREHENSION 1   **Decide if the sentences about the people are True (T) or False (F).**

1   They all read magazines.   Y ☐   N ☐

2   Two of them look at the Internet.   Y ☐   N ☐

3   Nobody is reading any paperbacks in English.   Y ☐   N ☐

4   Only one person reads a newspaper.   Y ☐   N ☐

5   Five of them read something that's not on the list.   Y ☐   N ☐

6   The IT technician reads the most different kinds of things.   Y ☐   N ☐

COMPREHENSION 2   **Answer the questions.**

1   In lines 3 and 4, which sentence about the technician is correct?

   a   He has paid money to receive monthly copies of a gardening magazine.

   b   He sells a gardening magazine every month.

   c   His gardening magazine is free every month.

2   In line 5, what does *articles* mean?

   a   *the*, *a*, or *an*

   h   small objects

   c   pieces of writing in a newspaper or magazine

3   In line 8, another way of saying *to start doing something regularly as a habit* is _____.

4   In lines 11 and 12, what does *features on golf courses* mean?

   a   free passes to play on a golf course

   b   newspaper or magazine articles on golf courses

   c   advertisements in a newspaper or magazine for golf courses

5   In line 12, which information does the housewife get about the latest golf equipment?

   a   someone's opinion

   b   the history of the product

   c   how much it costs to make

6   In line 14, which phrase means *having the most recent news and information*?

7   In lines 25 and 26, why does the student read the horoscopes?

   a   to find out which of her male friends are always correct

   b   to find out if any of her friends will meet their perfect man

   c   to find out if any of her friends will meet a right-handed man

8   In line 27, which phrase shows that buying a lot of *manga* magazines is expensive?

9 In lines 29 and 30, what does the student have in his notebooks?

   a notes about what his lecturers have said

   b detailed drawings

   c drawings made very quickly

10 In line 33, which phrase means *not including something*?

COMPREHENSION 3 **Find the four verbs in the text; they are all different ways of reading. Then match a verb with a definition.**

1 look something up

2 browse

3 skim

4 study

a to read something quickly and not very carefully

b to spend time learning about a subject by reading

c to find a piece of information by looking in a book or on a computer

d to look at information or pictures in a book without looking for anything in particular

Now do the same with these.

1 read up on something

2 read something out

3 skip

4 scan

a to read something quickly to find particular information

b to intentionally miss pages or paragraphs when reading

c to get information on a particular subject by reading a lot about it

d to say the words that you are reading so that people can hear them

COMPREHENSION 4 <u>Underline</u> **the best verb to complete the sentences.**

1 If you don't understand the word you can *look it up* / *browse* in a dictionary.

2 Don't worry about understanding everything. *Just study* / *skim* the text to get the general meaning.

3 The first chapter is not important so we'll *read* / *skip* that and go onto chapter two.

4 I haven't got my glasses with me, can you *read out* / *read up on* what it says here, please.

5 Your homework tonight is to *read up on* / *scan* your favourite author so you can tell the class about him or her tomorrow.

6 You have two minutes to *scan* / *browse* the text and tell me when and how the king died.

Grammar	An object pronoun replaces a noun:
Object and reflexive pronouns	*It helps* **me** *to relax.*
	They're really helping **me** *to improve.*
	A reflexive pronoun is usually used when the subject and object are the same:
	I'm teaching **myself** *French.*

GRAMMAR 1   **Are the pronouns in the sentences correct?**

For example:

Ouch! I've just cut myself with this knife. ✔

1   Do you have a mirror? I want to see me in this new hat.

2   'Can I have a biscuit?' 'Of course, help yourself!'

3   I really liked the party last night. I enjoyed me a lot.

4   Please wait! Don't go without myself. I'll be ready in two minutes.

5   'How did he die?' 'He shot himself.'

6   In an interview, the best thing to do is to just relax and be you.

GRAMMAR 2   **Complete the sentences with *me*, *myself*, *you*, or *yourself*.**

1   I'm going to make _____ work really hard to pass my exams.

2   Oh no! I forgot my mother's birthday! I really hate _____!

3   Are you OK? Did you hurt _____?

4   My uncle wrote _____ a letter inviting me to stay with him.

5   I feel unhappy so I'm going to buy _____ some chocolate.

6   You really love _____, don't you? You're always looking in the mirror!

7   If you want to stop smoking, I'll try and help _____.

8   I weighed _____ this morning – I've lost 3 kilos!

GRAMMAR 3   **Which of these opinions do you agree with? Explain why to another student.**

1   Magazines are just for fun; they're not for serious reading.

2   Comics are only for children.

3   It's much easier to read newspapers and magazines than to read articles on the Internet.

4   Reading paperbacks is boring. I much prefer watching TV.

5   Graded readers are interesting and fun to read.

Effective • *Skills*

Read a short passage from the first chapter of a graded reader set in the Middle East

> 'Can I help you?' said the manager.
>
> 'Yes,' replied Salahadin. 'My name's Salahadin El Nur. I'm a police inspector. I want to speak to Mr Pearson.'
>
> 'Do you mean Mr Pearson, the archeologist?' asked the manager.
>
> 'Yes,' replied Salahadin.
>
> 'I'm sorry. You can't speak to Mr Pearson, sir,' said the manager.
>
> 'Oh?' said Salahadin in surprise. 'Why not?'
>
> 'Mr Pearson is dead,' replied the manager. 'He was found dead in his room this morning …'

What kind of story do you think it will be? You can choose more than one answer.

1	Horror	**5**	Detective	**9**	Travel
2	Romance	**6**	Adventure	**10**	Thriller
3	Mystery	**7**	Spy		
4	Ghost	**8**	Science Fiction		

Now read part of the story.

The road to Ba'albek

The black car moved a few metres and stopped again behind a shed. Fuad and Salahadin sat and waited. Borkman got off the boat and got into a taxi. The taxi started to move away.

5   'Let's follow him,' said Fuad.

'Wait a moment,' said Salahadin. 'Watch the black car.'

Salahadin was right to wait. The black car pulled out slowly and followed Borkman's taxi.

10   'We can set off now,' said Salahadin. 'We'll follow the black car. There's something strange going on here.'

The road to Ba'albek is taken from *The Black Cat* by John Milne, a title from the Macmillan Readers series. Text © John Milne 1975

The Black Cat
John Milne

15

The three cars drove out of the docks, one after the other. The taxi went quickly through the streets of Beirut. Then it started to climb the steep road towards the mountains. The black car followed the taxi. Fuad followed the black car.

'Isn't this the road to your village?' asked Salahadin.

'Yes,' replied Fuad. 'This road goes higher up into the mountains. It goes to a small town called Ba'albek.'

20

'I've heard of Ba'albek,' said Salahadin. 'There are some famous ruins there.'

'And there's a gang of smugglers, too,' said Fuad. 'They smuggle antiquities out of Beirut.'

The three cars drove up the steep road. They went past Fuad's village.

25

Fuad drove on in silence. The road became narrower and steeper, so Fuad kept away from the black car.

'The road's more dangerous here,' said Fuad. 'There was an accident a few weeks ago. Four people were killed.'

For a few moments nothing happened.

30

Then the black car began to go faster. It had moved into the middle of the road and was trying to pass Borkman's taxi. The two cars were now side by side. They were almost touching each other.

35

There was a sharp bend in the road in front of them.

'They'll never get round that bend!' shouted Fuad.

But it was already too late. There was a

40

loud crashing noise. Fuad slowed down and drove carefully round the bend. The black car and the taxi had disappeared. The road was empty in front of them. Everything was silent.

GENERAL UNDERSTANDING

Decide if the sentences are True (T), False (F) or if the text Doesn't Say (DS).

1 Borkman is in the first car.   Y ☐ N ☐ DS ☐

2 Both Fuad and Salahadin are police officers.   Y ☐ N ☐ DS ☐

3 Fuad is driving.   Y ☐ N ☐ DS ☐

4 Fuad lives in Ba'albek.   Y ☐ N ☐ DS ☐

5 The first two cars had an accident and drove off the road.   Y ☐ N ☐ DS ☐

6 Borkman is dead.   Y ☐ N ☐ DS ☐

VOCABULARY IN CONTEXT 1

Match a word or phrase in the text to the definitions.

For example:

a small simple building used for keeping things in	*shed, line 1*
1 to go after or behind somebody	_____
2 rising or falling quickly (connected to a hill)	_____
3 parts of a building that remain after it has been badly damaged	_____
4 people who take things into or out of a country illegally	_____
5 things which are very old	_____
6 a curve or turn, especially in a road or river	_____

VOCABULARY IN CONTEXT 2

There are a number of phrasal verbs in the reading:

Borkman *got off* the boat.   The taxi started to *move away*.

Choose the correct phrasal verb for the following sentences. Read again to check your answers.

1 The black car pulled *out / in* slowly and followed Borkman's taxi.

2 'We can set *off / in* now,' said Salahadin.

3 There's something strange going *around / on* here.

4 Fuad drove *under / on* in silence.

5 The road became narrower and steeper, so Fuad kept *away / up* from the black car.

6 Fuad slowed *up / down* and drove carefully round the bend.

SPEAKING

Ask another student these questions.

1 Do you like reading detective stories or adventure books? If not, what kinds of books do you like reading?

2 What was the last book you read? What was it about?

3 Which countries produce some of your favourite books and films?

4 Do you have a favourite writer? If so, who is it and why?

PRONUNCIATION

Find the ten words in the text. Decide which consonant (or consonants) in each word is silent.

1 car	**4** through	**7** few	**10** sharp
2 metres	**5** climb	**8** four	
3 follow	**6** town	**9** two	

EXERCISE 1

Read the text.

Jump for joy!

Joy: I like difficult sports. I (1) _____ paragliding and kitesurfing and really loved them. So last weekend, I (2) _____ bungee jumping and it was wonderful! I jumped from a bridge that was 100 m high. Paul, my boyfriend, didn't want me to do it – he (3) _____ as I jumped. It was very safe, though. I was strapped into a (4) _____ and the organisers were all very (5) _____. I was a bit worried at first because in the morning it was raining. However, it (6) _____ a lovely day and there was a (7) _____ crowd watching. It's a (8) _____ pity that Paul didn't give it a try. Maybe next time!

EXERCISE 2

Choose a word or phrase to complete the paragraph. Use each word or phrase once only.

harness   great   experienced   turned into
went   huge   have tried   looked on in horror

EXERCISE 3

Complete the sentences using *but, because* or *so* to make true sentences about the text.

1 Joy likes difficult sports, _____ she decided to try bungee jumping.

2 Paul didn't want Joy to do it, _____ he didn't stop her.

3 He doesn't like bungee jumping _____ he thinks it's dangerous.

4 Joy was safe _____ she was wearing a harness.

5 It was raining in the morning _____ in the afternoon the weather was nice.

6 Joy wants Paul to give it a try _____ he really doesn't want to!

EXERCISE 4

Decide in which words the underlined *-ed* ending is pronounced like:

\t\ watch<u>ed</u>   \d\ smil<u>ed</u>

1 tri<u>ed</u>

2 lov<u>ed</u>

3 jump<u>ed</u>

4 look<u>ed</u>

5 strapp<u>ed</u>

6 experienc<u>ed</u>

7 worri<u>ed</u>

8 turn<u>ed</u>

Review | Unit 12

EXERCISE 1 Music mags

Read the text.

Sasha: I play in a band and like to read about music and other bands, too. I have a monthly **subscription** for *The Sound* but I also buy other magazines if I see they've got any interesting **articles** on musicians I like. I spend hours in bookshops **browsing** the music section and **flipping through** the pages of magazines I can't afford to buy. When I want to get a new guitar, I usually use the Internet to **read up on** the latest models. There are some great **websites** with **reviews**, as well as tons of **advertisements**. I don't really read anything else, apart from music, of course!

EXERCISE 2

Decide if the answers are Yes (Y), No (N), if the text Doesn't Say (DS).

1 Does Sasha buy music magazines because he wants to become a musician?

  T ☐ F ☐ DS ☐

2 Does he spend a lot of money buying magazines?

  T ☐ F ☐ DS ☐

3 Does he sometimes look at magazines in bookshops but not buy them?

  T ☐ F ☐ DS ☐

4 Does he use the Internet for information about guitars?

  T ☐ F ☐ DS ☐

5 Does he buy his guitars through the Internet?

  T ☐ F ☐ DS ☐

6 Can he read music?

  T ☐ F ☐ DS ☐

EXERCISE 3

Complete the sentences with a word or phrase in bold from the text.

1 I don't like reading newspapers. The _____ are always about bad things.

2 'What book are you looking for?' 'Nothing, I'm just _____.'

3 I really want to see the latest Bond film; it's got great _____.

4 There are many _____ on the Internet to help people learn English.

5 I don't have to worry about my favourite magazine selling out. I have a _____ and it's sent to my home each month.

6 I'm going to the library to _____ Mozart. We've got an exam on him next week.

7 The first part of a fashion magazine always contains _____, often for perfume and make-up.

8 At the dentist I was only _____ the pages of the magazines. I was too nervous to read anything in detail!

Introduction

About the author

The Legend of Sleepy Hollow is taken from *The Legends of Sleepy and Rip Van Winkle* by Washington Irving, a title from the Macmillan Readers series. Text © Anne Collins 2000

Washington Irving was an American writer. He was born on April 30th, 1783, in New York. As a young man, he studied law and he worked in several law firms. But from 1802, he also wrote stories and essays. At first, these were published in newspapers, but later they were collected and published in books.

During the years 1804-06, Irving travelled in Europe. He left the United States again in 1815, and he lived in Europe for many years. At first, he worked for a company which was owned by his two brothers, in Liverpool, in England. Eleven years later, he went to live in Madrid, in Spain. He worked for the United States government there. After that, he returned to England for several years, and in 1832, he went back to the United States. His books were now very popular there.

During 1842-46, Irving worked in Madrid again. This time he had a more important government job. Then he returned for the last time to the USA. He lived in a beautiful house in Tarry Town (Tarrytown), near New York, until his death in 1859.

Irving was the first great American writer of humorous stories. He also wrote books about the countries he visited, and a book about the life of George Washington – the first president of the USA.

The Legend of Sleepy Hollow first appeared in *The Sketch Book*, Irving's most popular book, which was published in 1820.

About the story

Dutch people arrived in North America from the Netherlands early in the seventeenth century. They came to live in a new land – they were settlers. Many of them made their homes in the area around the Hudson River, in the east of the land. But nearly two hundred years later, this part of North America was a British colony. The land was owned by Britain. The colony was ruled by King George the Third, who was the British king from 1760 to 1820. Some people in North America were happy about this. They liked the British king – they were loyal to King George. But many others did not want their land to be ruled by Britain. They wanted to live in an independent country. They wanted their own government and they wanted their own laws. There was a war between these people and the British army. The Americans won the war, and the British left the colony. The colony became the United States of America. The country has a president, not a king. The first president of the United States was George Washington.

The Legend of Sleepy Hollow takes place after the war with Britain, early in the nineteenth century.

The Legend of Sleepy Hollow

1 *The Ghost of the Soldier*

On the eastern bank of the great Hudson River, in North America, there is a small town. Its name is Tarry Town. Once the town had a different name. Why did it change? This is the reason. Wives often sent their husbands to the market in the town to buy and sell things. 'Come back quickly,' the wives always said. But the husbands never returned home quickly. They stayed or 'tarried' in the town and they drank beer at the inns there. So people started to call the place Tarry Town.

About two miles from Tarry Town is a little hollow – or valley – between some high hills. A small river runs through this valley. The valley is a very peaceful place. Everyone who goes there soon feels peaceful. They quickly forget their troubles. And everyone who lives there always feels sleepy. Because of this strange peaceful feeling, the valley is called 'Sleepy Hollow'.

Dutch settlers first came to Sleepy Hollow early in the seventeenth century. They made their homes there. But before the Dutch people came, Native Americans had lived there. These people believed in many different spirits. Perhaps these spirits made Sleepy Hollow a strange and mysterious place.

There was something very strange about the people who lived in Sleepy Hollow in the early years of the nineteenth century. They were as peaceful and as sleepy as the valley itself. They believed strongly in God. But they also believed very strongly in ghosts and spirits. They often saw strange things at night. They often heard music in the forest when nobody else was there.

There were many stories about ghosts and spirits in Sleepy Hollow and the area near it. The most famous of these stories was about the ghost of a man on a horse. Lots of people saw the man – that is what they said. He rode a huge black horse, as fast as the wind. He was always seen late at night. And there was something even more terrible about him. He had no head! So the people who lived in the area called him, 'The Headless Horseman'.

Many people had seen the Headless Horseman late at night. He rode in Sleepy Hollow and he also travelled on the other roads in the area. He was often seen near a small church, a few miles from the valley.

Who was this Headless Horseman? Nobody really knew. But some people told a story about him.

'The Headless Horseman is the ghost of a soldier,' they said. 'This soldier was killed in the war between Britain and the American colony. There was a terrible battle in this area. In this battle, the soldier's head was shot off by a cannonball from a British gun.

'His body was taken to a little church near the battlefield,' these people continued. 'It was buried in the graveyard next to the church. But his head still lies somewhere on the battlefield. Every night, the Horseman rides back to the battlefield to look for his head. But he never finds it. And he always has to return to the graveyard before dawn. All ghosts have to go back to their graves before the daylight comes. And the Headless Horseman is always in a hurry because he's always late. That's why he rides so fast.'

2 *The Schoolmaster*

The schoolmaster of Sleepy Hollow was a man named Ichabod Crane. His name was a good one because he looked like the kind of bird which is called a crane. He was very tall and thin, with narrow shoulders and long arms and legs. His head was small, and very flat on the top. He had huge ears, large green eyes and a very long nose. He was not handsome at all.

Ichabod's clothes did not fit him well. They were loose, and they flapped in the wind. So when he walked, the schoolmaster looked very strange.

The school was a low building with one large room, and Ichabod was the only teacher there. This schoolhouse stood by itself at the bottom of the valley. The hills around it were covered with trees. A small river ran near the schoolhouse.

On summer days, the windows of the schoolhouse were always open. Anyone who passed could hear Ichabod's pupils saying their lessons in sleepy voices.

When lessons had finished for the day, Ichabod often went home with one of the children. Some boys and girls had pretty older sisters. Ichabod liked young, pretty ladies. And some of his pupils had mothers who were good cooks. Ichabod liked to go home with these children most of all.

Ichabod was very thin, but he ate a huge amount of food. He loved talking about food and he loved thinking about food. Most of all, he loved eating it.

Ichabod loved food, but he loved singing too. He taught a group of young people to sing psalms – religious songs. Once a week, the group met for psalm-singing lessons. And every Sunday, Ichabod stood with his pupils in the church in the valley and sang psalms with them.

Ichabod had a good life. He did not earn very much money from teaching. He could not buy a house of his own. So he stayed at the houses of different farmers in the area. He stayed with each farmer for a week. Each week, a farmer gave the schoolmaster a bed to sleep in and food to eat. And Ichabod helped the farmers with the work on their farms. He mended fences. He took water to the horses. He cut wood for the farmers' fires. Sometimes he helped the farmers' wives to look after their children.

The farmers' wives were always happy to see Ichabod. They often invited him to tea. They made delicious cakes for him. The young women of the area liked Ichabod too. Sometimes he took walks with them, or read them funny stories. They smiled at him whenever they met him.

All the people of Sleepy Hollow respected Ichabod Crane because he was a schoolmaster. He was clever – he worked with his mind, not with his hands. 'He's a very intelligent man,' everyone said. Most of the people in the valley could not read or write. But Ichabod *could* read. So he was an important man in the area.

Ichabod Crane believed in God, but he also believed very strongly in ghosts and spirits. On summer evenings, after lessons had finished, he often lay on the grass beside the small river. He lay on the warm grass and read his favorite book. It was a book about ghosts.

Ichabod loved the stories in this book, but they frightened him. He believed everything that he read in them! He often read the book until the sky was dark. Then he could no longer see the pages, so he stopped reading. But then he had to walk back in the dark, to the farmhouse where he was staying.

A forest covered a large part of the area. Often, Ichabod had to walk through the forest to get to the farmhouse. These walks in the dark were terrible for him. He saw ghosts and spirits all around him. The branches of the trees looked like ghostly hands. And they were all trying to grab him.

And there were strange noises in the forest at night. They were really the noises of animals and birds in the trees. But to Ichabod, they were the sounds of evil spirits. Sometimes, his heart beat fast with fear and his legs would not move.

'This is terrible!' he thought, whenever this happened. 'There are evil spirits here. They're hiding in the trees and they want to take me away with them. What can I do?

I'll sing a psalm. Then the spirits won't be able to hurt me.'

So Ichabod often sang a psalm as he walked through the dark forest:

> *I'm not afraid of ghosts*
> *or evil spirits of the night.*
> *God will always lead me*
> *from the darkness to the light.*

The people of Sleepy Hollow often sat outside the doors of their houses in the evenings. They heard the sound of Ichabod's strange, high voice as he passed their homes.

'What's that strange noise?' they asked each other. 'Is it a spirit? Oh, no, it's only Ichabod Crane. He's singing as he walks home through the forest!'

On winter evenings, Ichabod sometimes sat with the old women of Sleepy Hollow. He sat by their kitchen fires with them, eating apples and listening to their wonderful ghost stories.

Ichabod's favorite ghost stories were about the Headless Horseman. But when he had to walk home through the forest in the dark winter night, he tried to forget about the stories. He was even more frightened than in the summer.

'Does the terrible Horseman only travel on the roads?' he asked himself. 'Or does he haunt the forest too?'

On those dark nights, Ichabod saw the Horseman in every shadow. He heard the noise of the huge black horse in every sound!

3 *Ichabod and Katrina*

One day, a new pupil joined Ichabod's group of psalm-singers. Her name was Katrina Van Tassel, and she was the daughter of Baltus Van Tassel, an old farmer. Baltus Van Tassel's farm was a few miles from Sleepy Hollow.

Katrina was eighteen years old and she was very beautiful. She had golden blond hair and she liked wearing pretty clothes. All the young men in the area admired Katrina. And Katrina knew this. She enjoyed this admiration very much.

'Katrina is a very pretty girl,' said the people of the area. 'Her skirts are too short now! But one day, she will be a good wife for somebody. Her husband will be a very lucky man. He will marry Katrina and he'll get her father's farm too.'

Katrina was Baltus Van Tassel's only child. She had no brothers or sisters. So when her parents died, Katrina was going to inherit the farm. The land and every-thing on it was going to be hers. One day, she was going to be rich.

Ichabod Crane liked women. But when he first met Katrina, he forgot about all other women.

Soon after he met Katrina, Ichabod visited the Van Tassels' farmhouse. It stood in a wide, grassy place on the bank of the Hudson River. As Ichabod rode up to the farmhouse, he saw cows, geese, ducks, turkeys and hens. They all looked very fat and healthy.

At once, Ichabod began to feel hungry. He thought about huge and wonderful dinners.

'Those chickens will taste delicious when they are cooked,' he thought. 'And those geese and turkeys will be wonderful in pies. And the ducks will be very good with onions.'

Then Ichabod looked at all the land which belonged to the farm. He saw fields of golden corn. He saw hundreds of fruit trees, their branches covered with ripe fruit. And when Ichabod saw all these things, he started dreaming about his future life.

'This place is perfect,' he said to himself. 'If I marry Katrina, I'll have an easy life. I won't have to work. There'll be lots of delicious food all the time. Katrina will take good care of me. I'll be very comfortable here with her and our children.

'Perhaps we'll sell the farm one day,' he thought. 'We'll get a lot of money and then we'll travel to another part of America.'

Ichabod was happy. And when he entered the farmhouse, he felt even happier. The kitchen was large, warm and comfortable. There was a wonderful smell of food. There were large baskets full of fruit and vegetables, ready for cooking.

In the living room, the fine wooden furniture shone in the sunlight. The cupboards were full of silver plates and china dishes.

From that time, Ichabod thought day and night about Katrina. 'I must marry her,' he said to himself. 'There's a wonder-ful life waiting for me on that farm.'

4 Brom Bones

But there was a problem for Ichabod. All the young men from the area admired Katrina. And there was one young man who admired her very much. He wanted to marry her too. This man's name was Brom Bones.

Brom Bones was very different from Ichabod. He was tall and handsome. His body was big and strong, and he had short, black, curly hair. He was a very brave young man and he was an excellent horse rider. He often rode in horse-races and he always won them.

Brom Bones was not afraid of anybody or anything. He was the leader of a group of young men. These young men admired Brom and they rode with him everywhere. Sometimes the people of the area heard the sound of horses on the road late at night.

'That's Brom Bones and his friends!' they said to each other.

Brom Bones enjoyed playing tricks on people. He was not a bad man, but he liked to have fun.

Brom Bones often went to Baltus Van Tassel's farm to see Katrina. When other young men from the area saw Brom's horse outside the Van Tassels' farmhouse, they smiled sadly.

'Now Katrina won't speak to us,' they said. 'Brom will win her love easily. And we don't want to fight with Brom.'

So everybody else stopped trying to win Katrina's love – everybody except Ichabod Crane.

Ichabod was not worried about Brom Bones and his visits to Katrina. He started to visit her himself. And when the schoolmaster came to the house, Katrina's father smoked his pipe happily. Her mother sang while she did her work. They both smiled when Ichabod took walks with Katrina, or when he sat and talked with her outside the house. All the Van Tassels were happy.

But when Brom Bones heard about Ichabod's visits to Katrina, he was not happy.

'What!' he shouted. 'Is that ugly schoolmaster visiting Katrina? I'll fight him. I'll knock him down and put him on a shelf in his own schoolhouse!'

But Ichabod did not want to fight Brom. Brom was very strong and he could win any fight easily – Ichabod knew that. So the schoolmaster stayed away from Brom. This made Brom even more angry.

'I can't fight him with my hands because he won't come near me,' Brom said. 'So I'll try another way of fighting him.'

He started playing tricks on the schoolmaster. First, Brom and his friends got into Ichabod's schoolhouse one night. They moved all the furniture around. Ichabod was very frightened the next day.

'An evil spirit did this,' he said.

Next, Brom taught his dog to make a terrible noise. Then he waited outside the schoolhouse with the animal. Whenever Ichabod sang, the dog made this terrible noise. All Ichabod's pupils laughed.

One fine autumn afternoon, Ichabod was in the school-house with his pupils. Suddenly there was a knock at the door. When Ichabod opened it, he saw one of Baltus Van Tassel's servants outside.

'You are invited to a party tonight at the Van Tassel farm,' said the servant. 'Will you come?'

'Oh, yes!' said Ichabod. He was very happy and excited. He also felt very important. Katrina's parents had asked him to a party. So they really did like him. They wanted him to marry their daughter. That was good. And he was going to see Katrina at the party.

He sent his pupils home an hour early that day. They were very surprised by this. It had never happened before!

5   *The Party*

Ichabod spent a long time getting ready for the party. He had an old black suit of clothes. It was his only suit. He brushed it carefully. When Ichabod looked at himself in a mirror, he was very pleased.

'How handsome I look,' he thought. 'Tonight, I'll win Katrina's love – I'm sure of that. But I must have a fine horse to ride to the party. Where can I get one? Perhaps I can borrow a horse from Hans Van Ripper.'

Hans Van Ripper owned the farm where Ichabod was staying that week. Ichabod asked to borrow a horse from him. The farmer decided to play a trick on the school-master.

'Yes, you can borrow one of my horses, Ichabod,' he said. 'I'll lend you my best one.'

But when Ichabod saw the horse, he was very surprised. It was old and thin, and it had only one eye.

'Is *this* your best horse?' he asked the farmer.

'Yes,' replied Hans Van Ripper. 'He's very strong and he runs as fast as a bullet from a gun. His name is Gunpowder.'

Gunpowder *did* run fast. But he also had a very bad temper. Hans Van Ripper did not tell Ichabod about this. He pointed to the saddle on the horse's back.

'This is my best saddle,' the farmer said. 'Please take care of it.'

Ichabod climbed onto the expensive saddle, and he and Gunpowder started their journey to the Van Tassels' party. Ichabod and the horse were both very thin and they looked very strange together! Ichabod was not a good horse rider. He sat uncomfortably on Gunpowder's back. As he rode, he moved his long thin arms up and down, like a bird's wings. His loose black coat flapped in the wind. He looked like a huge black bird.

It was a beautiful autumn afternoon. The leaves on the trees were red and gold. As Ichabod rode along, he heard the sounds of birds singing. He rode through fields of golden corn, and fields of apple trees. He began to feel hungry. He began to think about cakes and pies.

At last, Ichabod arrived at the Van Tassels' farmhouse. The party had already started and many of the farmers from the area were there with their families. Everybody was dressed in their best clothes. Their clothes were very colourful and bright.

The most beautiful girl at the party was

Katrina. Everybody admired her. She was laughing and talking to the guests. Ichabod looked at her and he smiled.

But soon, the schoolmaster had an unpleasant surprise. Brom Bones was also at the party. He had come on his big black horse, Daredevil. Brom was standing in the middle of a group of his friends. He was telling stories in a loud voice. Everybody was laughing at his stories.

'Oh, no!' thought Ichabod. 'Why is *that* man here?'

When Brom Bones saw Ichabod, his face became angry. Ichabod hurried away, into the dining room. And when he entered that room, he forgot about Brom Bones at once. He even forgot about Katrina!

In the dining room, a great table was covered with all kinds of wonderful food. There were dishes of cooked meat. There were plates of cakes and pies. Ichabod started eating at once. As he ate, he looked around the room and smiled.

'One day, all this will be mine,' he thought.

At that moment, Katrina's father came towards him.

'Are you enjoying the party, Ichabod?' Van Tassel asked. 'Please eat as much as you want. We have plenty of everything.'

After the meal, nearly everybody danced. Ichabod liked dancing very much. When he danced, he moved his arms and legs very quickly. He looked very strange! But he did not know this.

'I'm a very good dancer,' he told himself.

Ichabod started dancing with Katrina. Soon, everybody in the room was staring at them. Some people began to laugh.

'How strange Ichabod looks,' they said to each other. 'Why does he dance in that way?'

Brom Bones did not dance. He sat by himself in a corner. He stared angrily at Katrina.

'Brom is jealous because Katrina is dancing with *me*,' thought Ichabod. 'That's good.'

After the dancing had finished, Ichabod

felt tired. He joined a group of people by the fire. They were telling stories to each other. Brom Bones was one of the group.

At first, the stories were about the war between Britain and its American colony. But then people started to tell ghost stories. Ichabod listened carefully. He was always very interested in ghost stories.

Several people from Sleepy Hollow were at the party. They started talking about the Headless Horseman.

'The Horseman is riding again,' said one man. 'Nobody had seen him for a long time. But this month, several people have seen him. Every night now, he rides from the graveyard and he doesn't come back until just before dawn.'

'Yes, that's right,' said another man. 'And did you hear about poor old Farmer Brouwer? He met the Headless Horseman on the road. The Horseman pulled Brouwer up onto his terrible black horse and he rode away with him. He rode until he got to the small bridge near the old church. Then the Horseman threw Farmer Brouwer into the river and he rode away, making a noise like thunder.'

Suddenly Brom Bones spoke.

'I've met the Horseman too,' he said. 'But I wasn't afraid of him. I'm a better horse rider than he is.'

'Did you *really* meet him?' someone asked excitedly. '*How* did you meet him? Tell us what happened.'

'I met him on the road one night,' replied Brom Bones. 'I asked him to race with me. So we raced our horses to the old church. But my horse, Daredevil, was faster than his horse. I won the race easily. And when we got to the bridge near the church, the Horseman disappeared in a flash of fire.'

'You were very brave,' said someone.

Ichabod listened to Brom Bones's story. Then he himself told a story, about

evil spirits in the forest. But it was not as interesting as Brom's story. And nobody said, 'You were very brave' to Ichabod.

At last, the party finished, and it was time to go home. Ichabod went to find Katrina. He wanted to spend a few minutes alone with her.

'You're looking very beautiful tonight,' he told the young woman. 'May I come to see you tomorrow afternoon? I want to speak to you about something very important. I want to ask you a question.'

But Katrina did not look very happy or friendly. She did not want to be alone with Ichabod.

'No, I'm sorry,' she said. 'I won't be at home tomorrow afternoon.'

Ichabod was surprised. 'Oh!' he said. 'May I come tomorrow evening then?'

'No, I won't be here in the evening either,' Katrina replied.

'Well, can I come the next day?'

'No, I'll be busy all this week,' said Katrina. 'Now please excuse me. I have to say goodbye to our other guests.'

A few minutes later, Ichabod saw Katrina with Brom Bones. They were talking together and laughing quietly. Then Brom Bones held Katrina's hand and kissed it. Katrina was looking very pleased and happy.

'What *is* happening?' Ichabod asked himself. 'Does Katrina really like Brom Bones more than me? That's not possible! I

can't believe it! Perhaps she wants to make me jealous.'

Ichabod did not say goodbye to Katrina. He left the party quickly. He felt very sad, and he felt very angry too. He went to the stable – the place where the horses were kept – and he found Gunpowder. Gunpowder was asleep. But Ichabod kicked the horse and it quickly woke up.

Ichabod climbed onto Gunpowder's back and he rode slowly away

6   *A Terrible Race*

It was almost midnight. The moon was shining brightly. Ichabod rode Gunpowder slowly along by the side of some high hills. Below him, on the other side of the road, he could see Tarry Town, on the bank of the wide, dark Hudson River. He could hear the sound of a dog barking on the other side of the river. But the sound was very far away, like a sound in a dream.

As he rode along, the schoolmaster remembered the ghost stories that people had told at the Van Tassels' party.

Suddenly, a cloud covered the moon. Ichabod felt lonely and afraid. In front of him, a huge tree stood by the side of the road. There was a very sad story about this tree. During the war between Britain and the American colony, a British soldier had hidden in this tree. His name was Major André. The man was a spy, and he was hiding from some American soldiers. Later he was captured and killed. Now, the people of the area called the tree, 'Major André's tree'.

'The tree is haunted by Major André's ghost,' a lot of people said.

Ichabod remembered this story, and his heart began to beat fast. He was afraid. He did not want to pass Major André's tree. But there was no other way for him to get home. So he began to sing loudly:

God will lead me safely
around this terrible tree.
No ghost or spirit
is going to frighten me –

Suddenly he stopped singing. He had heard a noise.

'What was that?' he asked himself. He looked up at the tree. Was something white hanging in it? Something white and terrible? Then he looked again. No, there was only a white mark on one of the branches.

'I'm dreaming,' he told himself. 'That noise was only the sound of the wind.'

Ichabod passed the tree safely. But now there was another danger. This danger was more terrible than the tree. There was a forest on one side of the road. And beyond the forest, there was a bridge over a little river. The American soldiers had captured Major André on this bridge.

'Sometimes, Major André's ghost haunts that bridge at night,' people said.

Ichabod wanted to ride quickly across the bridge. His heart was beating faster and faster. He kicked Gunpowder with both his feet.

'Come on, you stupid old horse,' he said. 'Move faster!'

But Gunpowder had a bad temper. He was not feeling happy. He did not *want* to cross the bridge. He stopped walking forwards. Instead, he turned off the road, into the forest. He ran into the forest for a few moments. Then he stopped very suddenly. Ichabod was not a good rider and he nearly fell off Gunpowder's back.

'Move, you stupid animal!' the schoolmaster shouted.

He shouted at the horse and he kicked it again and again. But Gunpowder did not move. The horse was looking at something in the forest. Ichabod looked too. His mouth became dry with fear.

A huge black shape was standing in front of him. What was it? Was it a ghost?

The hair on Ichabod's head stood up. His body shook. He wanted to escape, but the horse would not move.

'Who are you?' he whispered.

The thing did not answer.

'Who are you?' Ichabod asked again.

Still there was no answer. Ichabod began to sing loudly:

No evil thing can hurt me –

Suddenly, the thing moved. It moved out of the forest, and now it was in the middle of the road. Ichabod could see it more clearly. It had the shape of a large man on a huge black horse.

Then at last, Gunpowder decided to move. He ran back to the road. The horse ran towards the bridge. The strange Horseman waited. He did not move or speak. But when Gunpowder and Ichabod had passed him, he started to move too. He began to follow them. In a moment, he was beside them! They crossed the bridge together.

As Ichabod rode along, the Horseman rode beside him. When Ichabod rode quickly, the Horseman rode quickly. When Ichabod rode slowly, the Horseman rode slowly. He never left Ichabod's side. It was like a terrible race.

In a moment, the Horseman was beside them!
They crossed the bridge together.

Ichabod and the Horseman rode up a hill. Suddenly, the Horseman was in front. But at the top of the hill, he stopped his horse and waited. Now Ichabod could see the Horseman's shape very clearly against the dark-blue sky. The Horseman had no head. He was carrying his head in his hands.

Now Ichabod was really terrified – he was very, very frightened. He rode away as fast as he could. But again the Headless Horseman followed him.

At last they reached a place where a small road turned down into Sleepy Hollow. Ichabod tried to make Gunpowder turn down into the valley. He kicked the horse, again and again. But Gunpowder did not turn. He ran on past the road that went down to Sleepy Hollow.

'You stupid horse!' shouted Ichabod. 'We're going the wrong way!'

Ichabod could hear the sound of the Headless Horseman behind him. The Horseman was very close.

Suddenly, Gunpowder started to run faster. That was good! But it was very difficult for Ichabod to stay on the horse's back. And at that moment, the saddle broke and it fell away from the horse. Now Ichabod had to ride without a saddle. But somehow, he held on to the horse's neck.

'That was Hans Van Ripper's best saddle,' Ichabod thought. 'He'll be very angry with me. But I can't worry about that now. I must escape from this terrible Headless Horseman.'

The terrible race went on. Suddenly, through an opening between the trees, Ichabod saw the walls of a building. The building was near the road. Its walls were white in the moonlight. It was an old church.

'That's the church where the Horseman's body is buried,' thought Ichabod.

Just in front of the church, the road crossed a bridge over a river. Ichabod remembered the stories that he had heard at the Van Tassels' party.

'The Horseman left Brom Bones at the bridge,' the schoolmaster thought. 'He left Farmer Brouwer there too. So if I can reach the bridge, I'll be safe. The Horseman can't pass the bridge near the church. He'll leave me and he'll go back to the graveyard.'

Ichabod kicked Gunpowder again. Gunpowder ran forward across the bridge, and after a moment they had reached the other side. Was the Horseman still behind him? Ichabod turned around.

He saw the Headless Horseman standing up on his horse. He had lifted his arm in the air. He was going to throw something at Ichabod. He was going to throw his head!

Ichabod screamed as something hit him. It made a terrible soft sound. The schoolmaster fell off the horse and lay on the ground. As he lay there, the Headless Horseman passed by him, riding as fast as the wind.

7 *What Happened to Ichabod?*

The next morning, Gunpowder was found without his saddle. The horse was quietly eating grass in a field near Hans Van Ripper's farm. But there was no news of Ichabod Crane.

Ichabod's pupils waited at the schoolhouse all morning. But the schoolmaster did not come. The boys and girls were happy to miss their lessons. They ate apples and they played on the grass near the river.

By the afternoon, Hans Van Ripper began to worry about Ichabod.

'What's happened to him?' he asked himself. 'And where's my best saddle?'

Hans Van Ripper went to find some men from the village.

'The schoolmaster has disappeared,' he told them. 'We must try to find him.'

The men looked for Ichabod for a long time, but they could not find him. At last, they went to the old church by the bridge. They found some marks in the road. They were the marks made by two horses. The marks continued across the bridge, then they disappeared in the grass.

'Look!' said one of the men suddenly. 'There's the schoolmaster's hat.'

Ichabod's hat was on the road near the bridge. Beside the hat, there was a very large, soft pumpkin. The big, round, yellow fruit was about the size of a man's head. It was broken.

The water in the river was very black and deep near the bridge. Hans Van Ripper looked at it sadly.

'Ichabod couldn't swim,' he said. 'Perhaps he fell off my horse and drowned in the deep water. We'll look for his body in the river. But why is that pumpkin here? It's very strange.'

The men looked in the river, but they could not find Ichabod. At last, they all went home. Later in the day, Hans Van Ripper searched through Ichabod's things. The schoolmaster had owned two shirts, two pairs of shoes, one pair of pants, a very old book of psalms, and a book of stories about ghosts and spirits. Hans also found some poems about Katrina Van Tassel which Ichabod had written. None of these poems was finished.

Hans Van Ripper immediately threw the poems and the book of ghost stories into his kitchen fire.

'I'm never going to send my children to school again,' he said to his wife. 'They don't learn anything good there. They learn about ghosts and spirits and they learn foolish poetry.'

Soon, everybody in Sleepy Hollow had heard the story of Ichabod Crane's strange disappearance. People could not stop talking about it. What had happened to Ichabod?

Groups of people met together at the bridge by the little church. They pointed at the place where the schoolmaster's hat had been found. They remembered the stories about the Headless Horseman.

'Do you remember old Farmer Brouwer's story?' one of them asked. 'And Brom Bones's story too? They both met the Headless Horseman on this road. But he left them at the bridge. Perhaps Ichabod Crane met the Horseman too. Perhaps the Horseman captured him and carried him away.'

Ichabod had no family, and he did not owe money to anybody. So the people of Sleepy Hollow forgot about him quickly.

Near the hat, there was a very large, soft pumpkin.

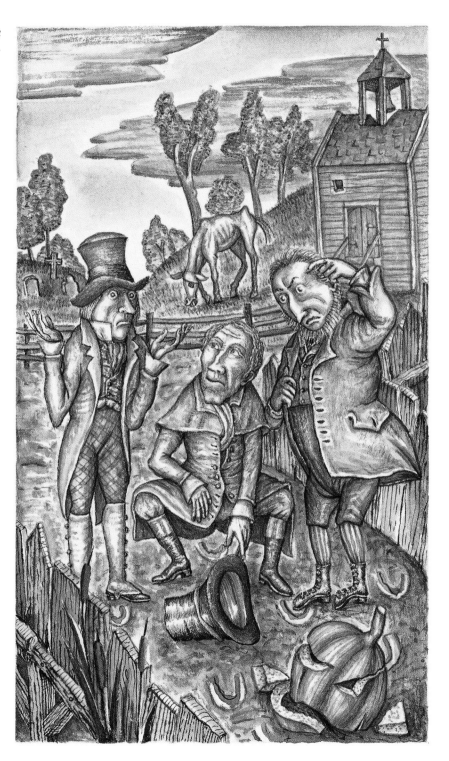

Soon, another teacher came to take Ichabod's place.

———

What really happened to Ichabod Crane? The old women of Sleepy Hollow knew the answer – they were sure of that. They often told the story of Ichabod when they sat by their fires on cold winter evenings.

'Ichabod Crane was taken away by the Headless Horseman,' they said. 'Nobody has seen him since that night. Nobody will ever see him again.'

People became very afraid of the bridge near the church. They said, 'This place is haunted by Ichabod's ghost. His ghost haunts the schoolhouse too. Some people have heard a voice singing strange songs and psalms there.'

On quiet summer evenings, people did sometimes hear strange sounds near the schoolhouse.

'Listen! Ichabod Crane is singing again,' they said. 'Or is it only Brom Bones's old dog?'

But there was another story about Ichabod Crane. Many years after Ichabod's disappearance, a farmer from Sleepy Hollow went to New York City. When he came back, he brought some very strange news.

'Ichabod Crane is alive,' the farmer said. 'I saw him in New York. I talked to him. He's a lawyer there. He's earning a lot of money.'

'What do you mean?' asked another man. 'Ichabod Crane is dead. He was taken away by the Headless Horseman.'

'No,' said the farmer. 'He left Sleepy Hollow secretly – he told me that himself. He was afraid of the Headless Horseman. And he was afraid of Hans Van Ripper, because he'd lost Hans's best saddle. He was also very angry, because Katrina Van Tassel had been unkind to him. So he did not want to stay here any more.

'Ichabod went to New York and taught in a school there,' the farmer went on. 'But he wanted to become a lawyer. So he studied law in the evenings.'

'Is this man's story true?' the people of the valley asked each other. 'Is Ichabod Crane really still alive?'

Perhaps only one person in the area knew the truth about Ichabod.

Soon after the schoolmaster disappeared, Brom Bones married Katrina Van Tassel. They were very happy together and they had many children. Whenever people talked about Ichabod Crane, Brom Bones always laughed loudly. He laughed loudest when they talked about the broken pumpkin.

Sometimes Brom's friends asked him about the night of the party.

'Do you know what really happened to the school-master, Brom?' they said. 'Please tell us!'

But Brom only laughed louder. *Did* he know what really happened that night? *Did* he know a secret about Ichabod and the Headless Horseman? Perhaps he did!